Practical Hexo

A Hands-On Introduction to Building Blogs Using the Hexo Framework

Alex Libby

Apress®

Practical Hexo: A Hands-On Introduction to Building Blogs Using the Hexo Framework

Alex Libby
RUGBY, UK

ISBN-13 (pbk): 978-1-4842-6088-3   ISBN-13 (electronic): 978-1-4842-6089-0
https://doi.org/10.1007/978-1-4842-6089-0

Managing Director, Apress Media LLC: Welmoed Spahr
Acquisitions Editor: Louise Corrigan
Development Editor: James Markham
Coordinating Editor: Nancy Chen

Cover designed by eStudioCalamar

Cover image designed by Freepik (www.freepik.com)

Distributed to the book trade worldwide by Springer Science+Business Media New York, 1 New York Plaza, New York, NY 10004. Phone 1-800-SPRINGER, fax (201) 348-4505, e-mail orders-ny@springer-sbm.com, or visit www.springeronline.com. Apress Media, LLC is a California LLC and the sole member (owner) is Springer Science + Business Media Finance Inc (SSBM Finance Inc). SSBM Finance Inc is a **Delaware** corporation.

For information on translations, please e-mail rights@apress.com, or visit http://www.apress.com/rights-permissions.

Apress titles may be purchased in bulk for academic, corporate, or promotional use. eBook versions and licenses are also available for most titles. For more information, reference our Print and eBook Bulk Sales web page at http://www.apress.com/bulk-sales.

Any source code or other supplementary material referenced by the author in this book is available to readers on GitHub via the book's product page, located at www.apress.com/9781484260883. For more detailed information, please visit http://www.apress.com/source-code.

Printed on acid-free paper

This is dedicated to my family, with thanks for their love and support while writing this book.

Table of Contents

About the Author

Alex Libby is a front-end engineer and seasoned computer book author from England. His passion for all things open source dates back to the days of his degree studies, where he first came across web development, and has been hooked ever since. His daily work involves extensive use of JavaScript, React, HTML, and CSS to create front-end UI components. Alex enjoys tinkering with different open source libraries to see how they work. He has spent a stint maintaining the jQuery Tools library and enjoys writing about open source technologies, principally for front-end UI development. You can find him on LinkedIn: `https://www.linkedin.com/in/alexlibby1/`.

About the Technical Reviewer

Kenneth Fukizi has over 14 years of experience in information technology–related services, 8 years committed to commercial software development through world-class independent software vendors. He is a co-founder of the AfrikanCoder project, a technology hub in Africa.

Acknowledgments

Writing a book can be a long but rewarding process; it is not possible to complete it without the help of other people. I would like to offer a huge vote of thanks to my editors – in particular, Nancy Chen and Louise Corrigan. My thanks also to Kenneth Fukizi as my technical reviewer and James Markham for his help during the process. All four have made writing this book a painless and enjoyable process, even with the edits!

My thanks also to my family for being understanding and supporting me while writing – I frequently spend lots of late nights writing alone, so their words of encouragement have been a real help in getting past those bumps in the road and producing the finished book that you now hold in your hands.

Introduction

Practical Hexo is for people who want to quickly create blogs that are efficient and fast, using nothing more than standard markdown and JavaScript code.

This project-oriented book simplifies the process of setting up Hexo and manipulating content, using little more than a text editor and free software. It will equip you with a starting toolset that you can use to develop future projects, incorporate into your existing workflow, and allow you to take your websites to the next level.

Over the course of this book, I'll take you on a journey through using the framework, showing you how easy it is to quickly create blogs. With the minimum of fuss, we'll focus on topics such as creating markdown content, turning it into valid blog posts, and more – right through to creating a simple ecommerce site!

Hexo is based on JavaScript and Node.js, two of the biggest tools available for developers: you can enhance, extend, and configure Hexo as requirements dictate. With Hexo, the art of the possible is only limited by the extent of your imagination and the power of JavaScript and Node.js.

Practical Hexo gets you quickly acquainted with creating and manipulating blogs using a static site generator (SSG) approach. It's perfect for website developers who are already familiar with JavaScript and keen to learn how to leverage the Hexo framework. You may also be a developer for whom time is of the essence and simplicity is key; you need to produce efficient and properly optimized content in modern browsers using tools already in your possession.

CHAPTER 1

Getting Started

Cast your mind back to the 1990s. Anyone remember the likes of Usenet, CompuServe, bulletin boards, and the like? These online communities were very popular at the time and gave rise to what we now know as weblogs.

The term blog was coined back in December 1997 by the developer Peter Merholz on his site, Peterme.com – who would know how a subtle but important change in how weblog would be articulated would make such an impact on developers worldwide? He simply said "we blog," instead of "weblog," sometime during 1999, and the rest we say is history…

But I digress – time to come back to reality! Blogging as an activity has become extremely popular over the years, with people posting articles on a host of different subjects, from their daily diary through to recipes for making cakes and beyond. There are a host of different tools available to create blogs, such as WordPress, Joomla, or even online tools such as Wix.com – all are perfectly valid tools, and each serves its own purpose.

So, what's new…?

That is a good question – one might think that with all of the tools available, we wouldn't need to change the status quo, right? After all, we can spin up a WordPress site for free, and with only a modest outlay and plenty of time, we can begin to create our masterpiece.

Well, I hate to disappoint, but there are several good reasons why we need to change – they are:

- Simplicity
- Speed
- Security

1

© Alex Libby 2020
A. Libby, *Practical Hexo*, https://doi.org/10.1007/978-1-4842-6089-0_1

Okay, so the "triple-S" factor isn't something I've coined deliberately, but there is a good reason for this: current blogging tools just aren't as effective as they should be! Let me explain what I mean.

In this modern age of technology, customers are increasingly demanding speed and simplicity; the pressure is absolutely on us as developers to create apps that are performant and don't require an advanced degree in physics to work out how to use them! Blogging tools such as WordPress work very well in their own right, but are not the most efficient. I suspect a part of this is down to the amount of functionality they offer, but they also suffer from one other problem: databases.

Yes, odd as it may seem, but databases are an essential part of the architecture that makes up a blog; we need them to store information, yet a badly configured database can be slow and inefficient and increase the risk that our site will be hacked. So, what can we do? Is there an alternative?

Introducing Hexo

Absolutely! Let me introduce you to the world of static site generators (or SSGs), and – more to the point – one of them: Hexo! So, what are SSGs?

Put simply, SSGs take a set of markdown instructions and convert or transpile them into static sites. Gone are the days of having to communicate with databases; SSGs do away with them by default, which results in content that can be rendered faster, is more performant, and is equally more secure. Hexo is one such example of an SSG; all use similar techniques, but Hexo has been designed to focus specifically on creating blogs.

Hexo was originally introduced in 2012, by the developer Tommy Chen, and is available from `https://www.hexo.io` – since then, it has powered thousands of blogs worldwide, so has become very stable for production use. It's very easy to set up, with only two key software dependencies that have to be installed as part of the process. Let's take a look at what these are in detail, before we go ahead with setting up Hexo.

Some housekeeping tasks

So, we've been introduced to Hexo, but before we get stuck into setting it up and create our first blog, there is a little housekeeping we need to do! Don't worry, it's nothing onerous: we have to download a couple of packages, among other things. Let's take a look at what we need to do.

The first task is to make sure you have a decent text editor – I'm sure you will have something suitable already, but just in case you don't, then there are plenty of options available! Here are a few you can try:

- Atom is an open source cross-platform editor available from `https://atom.io`; it has Git control built in by default, which will be particularly useful for working with Hexo!

- You can also try out Visual Studio Code, available from `https://code.visualstudio.com/` – this is open source and works across Windows, Linux, and Mac platforms.

- If you prefer a commercial offering, then give Sublime Text a try – it is available for Windows, Linux, and Mac and can be downloaded from `https://www.sublimetext.com/3`.

Most editors will allow you to work with Hexo – it's a case of finding one you like the look and feel of and which fits in with your own development environment.

We will also need somewhere to host the files we generate: as you will see later, the content is already served via localhost, but this is intended to be in a development capacity. I would recommend availing yourself with a local web server such as Apache (this should already be available on Mac and Linux platforms by default); for Windows users, you can use something like WampServer (`https://www.wampserver.com/en/`), if you don't already have an existing local server installed and ready for use.

You can of course use any free web space, but you may not want to release content into the wild if it is publicly available!

Next up, we need to download Git for your platform – this is used to get packages such as starter themes or plugins:

- For Windows users, Git can be downloaded from `https://git-scm.com/download/win`.

- If you are a Mac user, you can install it using Homebrew, MacPorts, or the Git installer from `https://sourceforge.net/projects/git-osx-installer/`.

- For Linux users on Ubuntu or Debian, use this command: `sudo apt-get install git-core`.

We also need Node.js – we'll use this for a host of tasks, such as downloading and installing plugins and themes or creating build files for deployment. Node.js is available for download from `https://nodejs.org/en/download/` – you will need to download the relevant version for your platform.

I would recommend choosing the option marked "Recommended for Most Users" – this is sufficient for our needs.

Okay, we have our dependencies in place; let's move on and get everything installed and ready for use.

Getting the dependencies installed

We've downloaded our two dependencies for our platform, so it's time to get them installed – both are straightforward, but do require us working through a few steps, particularly with Git! Let's take a look at the steps needed in more detail, as part of our first exercise.

The instructions for each exercise will assume you are using Windows: this is the author's native platform. If you are using Linux or macOS as your preferred platform, you may need to adjust the steps to suit.

INSTALLING OUR DEPENDENCIES

To get started with installing Hexo, go ahead with these steps – I will assume you've downloaded the relevant packages as outlined earlier:

1. We'll begin by installing Git as an administrator. For this, go ahead and double-click the installer you've downloaded; click Yes to install.

2. Click Next and then Next again, to accept the default settings on the Select Components screen.

3. On the Choose the default Editor... screen, go ahead and pick which editor you want to use; then click Next.

The available options will depend on what editors you have installed – select the most appropriate for your platform.

---

4. On the next screen, choose the option "Git from the command line and also 3rd-party software"; then click Next.

5. On the Choosing HTTPS transport backend screen, choose Use the OpenSSL library; then click Next.

6. For the Configuring the line ending conversions, select Checkout Windows-style, commit Unix-style line endings; then click Next.

7. We're almost done. For the next screen, choose Use Windows' default console window; then click Next.

8. On the final selection screen, click the checkboxes on the top two options; then click Install.

9. Git will now install – once done, it will prompt you if you want to see the release notes. Deselect this checkbox, and then click Next, to close the installer.

10. We now need to install Node.js. Go ahead and double-click the installer; click Yes to accept the admin privileges.

11. When prompted, go ahead and click Next; then select the checkbox to accept the license terms.

12. Keep clicking Next to accept the default options and Finish at the end – this is sufficient for our needs.

Phew! We're done with setting up our development environment; time now for the all-important part: setting up Hexo! Thankfully, this is easier to install by comparison. Let's dive in and take a look at the steps we need to work through to get Hexo set up for use.

Installing Hexo

We're well on the way to getting our first blog set up – to install Hexo, we need to use the command line. It's a one-liner command which will make Hexo available across our entire PC. There is a good reason for doing this; before we explain why, let's get Hexo installed.

DEMO: INSTALLING HEXO

To get Hexo installed, follow these steps:

1. Fire up Node.js terminal session, then enter npm install hexo-cli -g, and press Enter.

2. It will run through the installation and end up with something similar to Figure 1-1.

```
Node.js command prompt                                    —   □   ✕

C:\>npm install hexo-cli -g
C:\Users\alexl\AppData\Roaming\npm\hexo -> C:\Users\alexl\AppData\Roaming\npm\nod
e_modules\hexo-cli\bin\hexo
npm WARN optional SKIPPING OPTIONAL DEPENDENCY: fsevents@2.1.2 (node_modules\hexo
-cli\node_modules\fsevents):
npm WARN notsup SKIPPING OPTIONAL DEPENDENCY: Unsupported platform for fsevents@2
.1.2: wanted {"os":"darwin","arch":"any"} (current: {"os":"win32","arch":"x64"})

+ hexo-cli@3.1.0
added 74 packages from 319 contributors in 8.762s

C:\>_
```

Figure 1-1. *Installing Hexo via the command line*

3. Leave the terminal session window open – we're going to make use of it very shortly, when we create our first blog.

For existing users of Node, you may spot that we've not created a package. json file; this is deliberate. This will be created later during the install process automatically; setting up a file now can result in NPM throwing an error.

At this stage, we now have Hexo installed. We're ready to create our first blog; that was painless, right? Creating a blog is equally easy to do. Let's take a look at the steps required in more detail.

Creating our first example blog

Okay, so we're ready to set up our first blog: for this, we'll use the name Hexo as our example. Don't worry at this stage if you're not entirely sure what's happening: we will absolutely go through everything, but for now, let's simply run through the steps to set up our blog as part of the next exercise.

CREATING OUR FIRST EXAMPLE BLOG

Go ahead and follow these steps to create our first blog:

1. First, revert back to the Node.js terminal session we had open from the previous exercise.

2. At the prompt, enter Hexo init myblog and press Enter, to create our first blog.

3. You will see various steps being performed (Figure 1-2) – when you see INFO Start blogging with Hexo!, enter cd myblog to change to the myblog folder, and press Enter.

```
npm                                                                    —    □    ×

C:\>hexo init myblog
INFO  Cloning hexo-starter https://github.com/hexojs/hexo-starter.git
Cloning into 'C:\myblog'...
remote: Enumerating objects: 30, done.
remote: Counting objects: 100% (30/30), done.
remote: Compressing objects: 100% (24/24), done.
Receiving objects:  62% (100/161)
Receiving objects: 100% (161/161), 31.79 KiB | 756.00 KiB/s, done.
Resolving deltas: 100% (74/74), done.
Submodule 'themes/landscape' (https://github.com/hexojs/hexo-theme-landscape.git) registered for path 'themes/landscape'

Cloning into 'C:/myblog/themes/landscape'...
remote: Enumerating objects: 1054, done.
```

Figure 1-2. Running through the install for our first blog...

4. At the prompt, enter npm install to set up our first blog – NPM will install some additional packages. You may see warnings from fsevents when running on Windows – fsevents is a Mac-only package, so these can be ignored.

7

5. At the prompt, enter hexo server and then wait a couple of moments; it will indicate that you can now browse to your first site – fire up your browser, and head over to http://localhost:4000 to see our site (Figure 1-3).

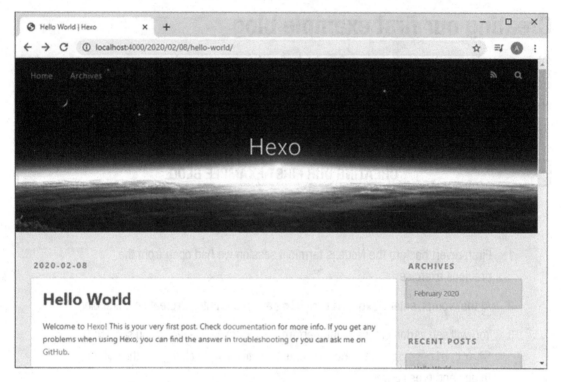

Figure 1-3. *Our first blog, up and running*

Congratulations if you made it this far. It might seem a lot, but trust me we only need to do the Git and Node.js installs once! With our two dependencies done, we only need to run the last part for any blog project we create.

In the meantime, we've run through what is arguably the most important part of working with Hexo – even though it looks relatively straightforward, it covers a few useful points that we should be aware, so let's dive in and take a look at what we've done in more detail.

Exploring the changes in detail

So, what did we do? It might seem a lot of steps, but as mentioned just now, most of them are only needed for the first time! Once that is done, then setting up a basic blog is a much quicker process. Let's take a look in more detail.

We kicked off by running through the install process for the two dependencies needed by Hexo, namely, Git and Node.js; we ran through the installation steps for Windows, but the choices will be similar for Linux and Mac platforms.

Next up, we then installed Hexo – we first installed Hexo as a global package, to allow us to create each blog site in separate folders. We then ran the `init` command to create our first blog and initialize the folder structure for it; this was completed by running the standard `npm install` to set up any missing dependencies. As the final step, we then ran the `hexo server` command to compile our code into static files and allow us to run the site in a browser window.

Okay, so we've built our first blog – granted, it's not going to win any style awards anytime soon, but hey, we must start somewhere! Trouble is I'll bet you're going to be a little unsure how all of this works, right? No problem – it's important to understand how Hexo works, so we can fine-tune it to our needs. With that in mind, let's dive in and take a look at the innards in more detail.

Understanding how Hexo operates

Now that we've built our first blog, do one thing for me – take a look at the compiled source. You can do this using Developer Tools in a browser – in Chrome, use Ctrl+Shift+I for Windows or Linux, or Cmd+Shift+I for Macs. Go ahead and have a look around, particularly at the Network tab. Have you noticed anything in particular?

Hopefully, you will see a site that appears to use standard HTML markup, and you might expect to see network calls to databases – in this case, you will definitely see the former, but not the latter! What gives…?

Well, we touched on how Hexo doesn't need databases by default – one of the ways it gets around not needing them is to use markdown files. These are just plain text files with the .md extension; Hexo uses these for content and YAML files for configuring each site. This is an important part of how Hexo works – to understand why, let's take a look at both the content and configuration files, starting first with content.

Breaking apart the folder structure

When we created our first blog, we set up a number of files and folders as part of the install process. Well, now would be a good time to take another look at the contents of our blog folder – go ahead and open it up in your file manager or explorer. Once open, you should see something akin to the screenshot shown in Figure 1-4.

Name	Date modified	Type	Size
node_modules	09/02/2020 11:16	File folder	
scaffolds	09/02/2020 11:14	File folder	
source	09/02/2020 11:14	File folder	
themes	09/02/2020 11:14	File folder	
.gitignore	09/02/2020 11:14	Text Document	1 KB
_config.yml	09/02/2020 11:14	YML File	3 KB
package.json	09/02/2020 11:14	JSON File	1 KB
package-lock.json	09/02/2020 11:15	JSON File	130 KB

8 items

Figure 1-4. *The folder (and file) structure of a Hexo blog*

Inside it, we can see a handful of folders and files. We have the typical `node_modules` folder which we get with any Node.js-based installation. I see a `package.json` there too, as well as three folders. What do they all do...? It's a good question. Let's start first with the folders.

Any Hexo blog will be made up of three folders (plus the standard `node_modules` folder) – they are all listed in Table 1-1.

Table 1-1. *The folder structure for a Hexo blog*

Folder name	Purpose
Scaffolds	This folder acts as a template for each new post you create and is used to create the post during processing.
Source	All content you add to a blog is stored in this folder; these files are used during the build and deployment process. The only exceptions are that they are marked as hidden, have an underscore at the start of the file name, or are in the _posts folder.
Themes	This stores the theme template for your site – it is used during processing when Hexo generates a static version of your site.

Hang on though. That's not all I see there. What about the files we mentioned just now? Yes, that's right. In addition, there are two files that are critical to the operation of any Hexo blog; they are `_config.yml` and `package.json`. The first takes care of configuring how your blog should be assembled; the latter contains the NPM dependencies required for Hexo to operate. Let's take a look at both in turn, starting with the _config.yml file.

You may also see a package-lock.json file appear too – this can be ignored. It contains an exact, versioned tree of dependencies, rather than the wildcard version you see in the standard package.json file.

The _config.yml file

The _config.yml file is where the magic happens – if you go ahead and open it up in a text editor, you will see something akin to the screenshot shown in Figure 1-5.

```
 5    # Site
 6    title: Hexo
 7    subtitle: ''
 8    description: ''
 9    keywords:
10    author: John Doe
11    language: en
12    timezone: ''
13
```

Figure 1-5. *An extract from our _config.yml file*

Inside this file, you will see a host of different settings – these are all used to configure our blog. In our case, we can see that our site's title is Hexo, the site's core language is English, and the author is named John Doe. Take a look at our blog from the previous demo – you will be able to see the site title top-center, with the author's name down near the bottom-left corner.

Using an alternative configuration file

In most instances, using a standard _config.yml file will satisfy our needs; however, it's worth noting that Hexo does allow us to use a custom configuration file if needed, using the --config flag.

To use it, we need to have either a YAML or JSON file (or it can be multiple files, in a comma-separated list **with no spaces**). We then run the hexo server command as before, but this time append the --config parameter, similar to the examples shown in the following:

```
# use 'myconfig.yml' in place of '_config.yml'
$ hexo server --config myconfig.yml

# use 'myconfig.yml' & 'myconfig2.json', prioritizing 'custom2.json'
$ hexo server --config myconfig.yml,myconfig2.json
```

The # symbol represents a comment line in YAML files and will be ignored when processed.

If we decide to use multiple configuration files, these are automatically merged together by Hexo into a _multiconfig.yml file. The important thing to note is that if the files contain duplicate settings, then the latter values take precedence. So, if we specified foo: bar in custom.yml, but "foo": "dinosaur" in custom2.json, _multiconfig.yml would contain foo: dinosaur.

Overriding a theme configuration

Although we talk about using _config.yml files as our means of configuring a site, in reality these are really config files for themes that we use in each project. This is perfect if we're running a single blog, but what if we're building multiple blogs?

The typical response would be to edit the config files for each blog as needed or potentially fork them and maintain our own custom settings, but that is time consuming, particularly if we're using similar settings across multiple blogs!

Instead, we can set up a primary _config.yml file and then override individual settings as needed in each project. It means we will need to maintain two configuration files per project, but this is a small price to pay when we can copy the overriding configuration file across multiple projects and only change those settings as needed. To see what I mean, take a look at this example:

```
# our primary _config.yml file, stored at the root of the blog
theme_config:
  bio: "My awesome bio"

# the overriding theme file, at themes/my-theme/_config.yml
bio: "Some generic bio"
logo: "a-cool-image.png"
```

This results in the following configuration settings:

```
{
  bio: "My awesome bio",
  logo: "a-cool-image.png"
}
```

We'll be taking a more in-depth look at tweaking our configuration file later in this chapter.

Okay, let's move on. The second file we need to concern ourselves with is the package.json file. Strictly speaking, this is not specific to Hexo, but a generic file that is used whenever Node.js is operating; that said, it is still worth a peek to see what kind of dependencies need to be present when operating a Hexo blog.

The package.json file

The package.json file is a standard part of a Node.js/NPM-based installation – this contains all of the dependencies used by Node when performing operations in a Hexo blog, such as starting the server or building the files for production use. If you open yours up, you should see something akin to the listing shown in Figure 1-6 (shown overleaf).

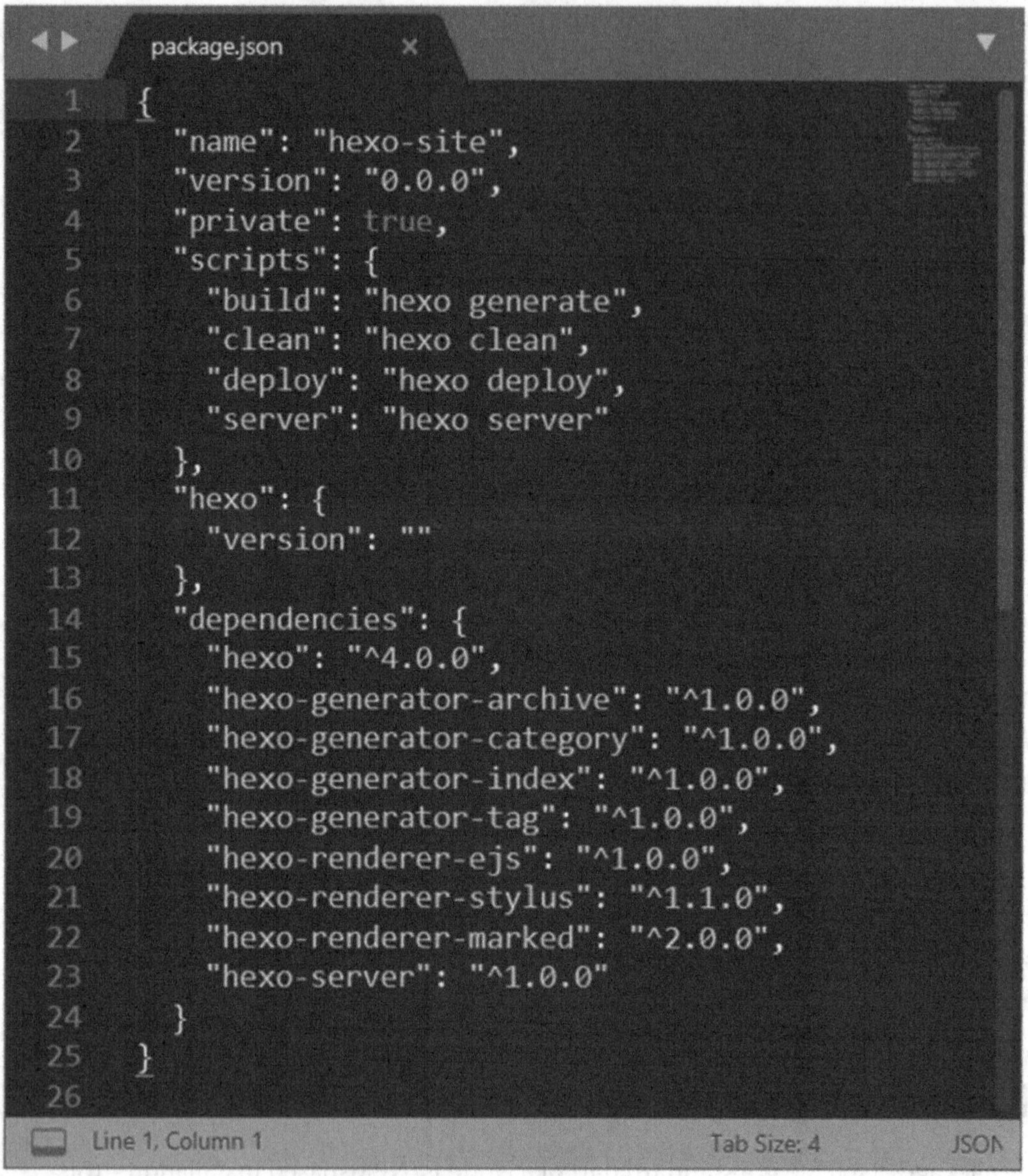

```json
1  {
2      "name": "hexo-site",
3      "version": "0.0.0",
4      "private": true,
5      "scripts": {
6          "build": "hexo generate",
7          "clean": "hexo clean",
8          "deploy": "hexo deploy",
9          "server": "hexo server"
10     },
11     "hexo": {
12         "version": ""
13     },
14     "dependencies": {
15         "hexo": "^4.0.0",
16         "hexo-generator-archive": "^1.0.0",
17         "hexo-generator-category": "^1.0.0",
18         "hexo-generator-index": "^1.0.0",
19         "hexo-generator-tag": "^1.0.0",
20         "hexo-renderer-ejs": "^1.0.0",
21         "hexo-renderer-stylus": "^1.1.0",
22         "hexo-renderer-marked": "^2.0.0",
23         "hexo-server": "^1.0.0"
24     }
25 }
26
```

Line 1, Column 1   Tab Size: 4   JSON

Figure 1-6. *The structure of our package.json file*

Our package.json file can be split into three parts. The first contains a number of
script commands that we use to generate files for production (build), reset the cache
and generated files (clean), deploy files to our server (deploy), or start the development
server (server). Any command that we run in this fashion must be prefixed with the
word hexo, for example, hexo server to start the development server.

The second section is used to display version information about the version of Hexo in use – we can run it in the same fashion as the commands at the top of the `package.json` file. It needs to be run when you have started the server – when executed, it will contain a list of version numbers, such as the `hexo-cli` package or the version of OpenSSL in use. Suffice to say it's not something you will need to use each day, but it's useful to operate if you find yourself stuck with an issue and need version information while debugging it!

The third and final part of the `package.json` file contains a number of generators, which are used as part of the build process. This includes the generators used for processing site content into static pages; by default, Hexo has three installed, which are EJS, Stylus, and Marked.

Okay, enough theory, methinks. It's time for action! We've covered some useful tips on the various features that make up our blog, so how about we put some of these into practice? Don't worry. It might at first look a little scary if you've not edited JSON files before; I'll take you through how to make the changes as part of the next exercise.

Changing our configuration

Making changes to the configuration of a Hexo blog is a key task for any blog we create – after all, not every site will have the same setup!

Most changes we make will be in either one of two files – the `_config.yml` file for each blog and the `package.json` file for any plugins we add into our site. We'll revisit the latter later in the book, but for now, we'll concentrate on how to make changes to the `_config.yml` file to fine-tune our blog's configuration.

We'll be covering a number of config changes as part of the upcoming exercise – if you would like to learn more about individual settings, please refer to the appendix at the end of this book.

Before we get started on our next exercise, there is something we need to be aware of – restarting our development server. This is typically needed when changes are made; it's a case of stopping a running process in a terminal session and reentering the hexo server command to restart. The important thing is to know when we need to restart – this will be when we are

- Editing the project's `_config.yml` file

- Installing or updating Hexo plugins with NPM

- Making changes to local plugins within the scripts folder(s)

In most cases though, our time will be spent authoring content in Markdown files; doing a hard restart shouldn't need to happen too often! With this in mind, let's turn to our next exercise, where we will begin to make changes to the configuration used by our blog.

UPDATING CONFIGURATION

Before we make any changes, we need to shut down our site if it is not already shut down; to do this, switch to the Node.js terminal session we have open, and press Ctrl (or Cmd) + C. Close your browser and any Node.js sessions you had open from the installation; then go ahead and follow these steps:

1. The first change we're going to make is to add in a description and subtitle – for this, open the `_config.yml` file at the root of our blog folder in your usual text editor.

2. Under the `#Site` entry, you will see several entries. Two of them will be `description` and `subtitle`; both will have empty values.

3. Go ahead and add in suitable text for both – I will use `"Creating blogs with the Hexo framework"` for the subtitle entry and `"Our first blog site made using Hexo"` for the description, but feel free to use something different if you prefer.

4. We're also going to add in some keyword tags – for this, look for the keywords entry, and add in `"test,hexo,blog"` as the value. You can add in more or others if you desire – they need to be comma separated, without any spaces between each tag.

5. At the same time, we'll change the author too – go ahead and replace "John Doe" against the author entry, with your own name.

6. I'm personally not a fan of the date format that has been used on this theme, so let's change it – scroll down to the date_format entry, and replace the value with MMM Do, YYYY.

Hexo uses the Moment.js date library to set dates – you can see more examples of date formats available at https://momentjs.com/.

---

7. Save the _config.yml file. There is one step left to do, which is to preview our changes. For this, fire up a Node.js terminal session, and change the working directory to our blog.

8. Next, enter hexo server at the prompt, and press Enter to start the Hexo server.

9. Go ahead and browse to http://localhost:4000, and you should see the site running – you can see two of the changes in Figure 1-7, with the updated date format and (highlighted) description.

Figure 1-7. *Our updated site*

10. For the other changes, fire up your developer console, and expand the `<head>` tag; you should see the keyword tags under `article:tag`, along with the updated author. For convenience, Figure 1-8 shows what the changes will look like for my version.

```
<meta name="description" content="Our first blog site made using Hexo">
<meta property="og:type" content="website">
<meta property="og:title" content="Hexo">
<meta property="og:url" content="http://localhost:4000/index.html">
<meta property="og:site_name" content="Hexo">
<meta property="og:description" content="Our first blog site made using Hexo">
<meta property="og:locale" content="en_US">
<meta property="article:author" content="Alex Libby">
<meta property="article:tag" content="test">
<meta property="article:tag" content="hexo">
<meta property="article:tag" content="blog">
<meta name="twitter:card" content="summary">
```

Figure 1-8. *Updated keyword tags and author details*

11. Keep your `_config.yml` file open for now – we're going to have a look at some bonus changes very shortly.

The changes we made in this exercise were very simple ones and required nothing more than adding in some text entries. There are a few more changes we could make that are a little more complex to add in. Let's take a look at two of them.

ADDITIONAL TWEAKS

For these changes, stop your server by pressing Ctrl+C in the Node.js window, then revert back to your `_config.yml` file, and follow these steps:

1. Hexo supports several different formats for blog permalinks – by default, this is set to `:year/:month/:day/:title/`, but we can do better! Go ahead and find the permalinks key in the `_config.yml` file; then change it to this:

    permalinks **:year/:month/:day/:title/**

There are more details on the permalinks page on the main Hexo site, at
`https://hexo.io/docs/permalinks`.

2. The next change we're going to make is to update the timezone – by default, this
    will be taken from the zone set on your PC. We can specify a value directly by
    editing the `timezone` key. Let's add one in now – for me it is `Europe/London`,
    but feel free to add in your timezone for wherever you are based in the world.

In case you're not sure of yours, check out the comprehensive list on Wikipedia, at
`https://en.wikipedia.org/wiki/List_of_tz_database_time_zones`.

Changing the URL of our blog

By default, any Hexo blog we create will run as localhost on port 4000 in a development
environment – for many, this will work absolutely fine. If you find that you need to
change this though, then no problem. Let's run through a summary of the steps to alter
the URL we use for our site:

- The first change is to make sure your Hexo server is shut down – as
  with any configuration change, we will have to restart the server for
  changes to take effect.

- Next, take note of the IP address you want to use – if you want to use
  a hostname, then make sure this is set up in your host file or on your
  DNS server.

- We then need to update the `_config.yml` file – look for the url: key,
  and alter the `url` value given to that of your new URL. You do not
  need to enter the port number; this will be taken care of when we
  restart the server.

- Once the `_config.yml` file has been updated, switch back to your
  Node.js terminal session, and then make sure the working directory
  is our blog (if it isn't already there).

- At the prompt, enter this command: `hexo server -i <your hostname> -p < your port number>`. Then press Enter.

- You should see confirmation that the server is now running – you can now browse to that URL, and if all is well, your site will be displayed using the new address.

This change only applies to hosting a site in a development/testing environment; we will explore how to host it as a custom production site later in this book.

Phew! We've been through a fair few changes there! We've only touched the surface of what is possible though; this is something we will revisit periodically over the course of this book as we begin to add content and media and improve our workflow process.

Although the changes we've made are straightforward, they nevertheless highlight some key points about how our blog site should be configured. To understand what I mean, let's pause for a moment to review those changes in more detail.

Exploring our code changes in detail

Over the course of the last demo, we made several changes to our configuration – we started by first adding in a description and subtitle for our site. We saw that any text can be added to the relevant keys, as long as it is enclosed in quotation marks. This was followed by adding in some keyword tags, before altering the author name to be our own.

The next change was to alter the default format used for dates – we touched on the fact that Hexo uses the Moment.js library and that any format available from this library can be used in Hexo. At this point, we previewed the first batch of changes, before moving on to explore how the permalink format can be updated and the site's timezone can be set. We also touched on how to reconfigure our blog site to be hosted via a different development URL, if we find ourselves needing to move it to an alternative location.

Summary

Blogging as an art is not new – it dates back to as far as the early 1990s, when individuals made use of CompuServe or bulletin boards as a precursor to what we now refer to as online blogs. Over the course of this chapter, we've explored how Hexo as a static site generator is changing this and the benefits it brings to the table. Let's take a moment to review what we've learned in this chapter.

We kicked off by setting a little historical background and discussing how tools such as Hexo are turning things on their head; we then moved onto installing Hexo as a tool and making sure it (and its dependencies) is set up for use.

Next up came a look at creating our first blog; we then took a look at how it works, before breaking apart the folder structure and exploring the various elements that make up a typical Hexo blog. We then rounded out the chapter by implementing some simple changes to our blog's configuration.

Okay, let's move on. We still have plenty to do! Now that we have a basic blog up and running, it's time to start adding content; we'll see how, as part of the next chapter.

CHAPTER 2

Manipulating Content and Media

With our initial blog set up, it's time to start adding content! Hexo doesn't use databases, but instead works with Markdown files; throughout this chapter, I will show you how easy it is to start adding and managing content, including images, sounds, and videos.

We'll also take a look at using tag plugins to help with formatting content such as code blocks or videos from external sources before preparing content for deployment at a later stage in our development process. There's plenty to cover, so let's crack on, starting with a quick overview as to how content is stored and structured within a Hexo blog.

Understanding how content is stored

Remember that I mentioned Hexo doesn't use databases by default, back in the previous chapter?

Well, without them, we need somewhere to store our content – enter Markdown files! One of the key constructs of Hexo is how it stores page, image, and post content; it is all stored within the _source folder at the top level of our blog site.

If you browse to this folder on your PC, you will see a folder structure similar to that shown in Figure 2-1.

© Alex Libby 2020
A. Libby, *Practical Hexo*, https://doi.org/10.1007/978-1-4842-6089-0_2

Figure 2-1. *Storing our content*

The first two highlighted are for drafts and posts, respectively; any pages we create are stored at the top level of the blog site, using the title of the page as its folder name and index.md as the file name within this folder. If we were to browse to the _posts folder, it would initially be empty; this will look something like Figure 2-2, once we add posts.

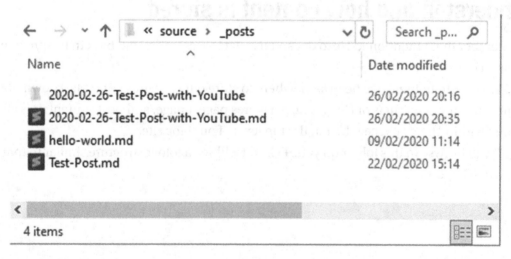

Figure 2-2. *Example post files in our blog*

Inside this folder, each file represents a post – by default, Hexo will use the title when creating each post as a markdown file. You will notice, though, that we have some additional folders here too; we use these to store images with each post, rather than in a central location.

This option is an alternative to using a central folder, which we'll explore in a later exercise.

Okay, now that we've taken a stroll through the basic folder structure of our blog, it's time to get creative! Yes, it's time for us to get down and dirty with code; we're going to work through adding each type of page content as part of the next exercise.

Creating written content

Adding posts and pages to a Hexo blog is very straightforward – we can do this with a single command, which we tweak based on the type of content we need to add:

```
hexo new [layout] <title>
```

We've already touched on the types of content we can add and where they are stored. By default, layout type is post, but we could substitute this for page or draft if we wanted to create a more in-depth article or not yet publish one. It's also worth noting that for posts we don't want to process, we can add `layout: false` into the front matter or head of each file.

We'll cover this layout trick in more depth, as part of an upcoming exercise.

Irrespective of the type of page that we're creating, Hexo will attempt to create it using a template type (or scaffold) from within the scaffolds folder. In this case, template type could be a little misleading as a description; it is simply a page format that Hexo will use when creating pages or posts in your blog.

Okay, with this in mind, let's dive in and put our newfound knowledge into practice; we're going to work through creating sample posts and pages using existing scaffold types, as well as creating a new one from scratch.

ADDING POSTS, PAGES, AND DRAFTS TO THE BLOG

To get started with adding posts and pages, go ahead with these steps:

1. First, we need to make sure our blog is running – if it isn't, then fire up two Node.js terminal sessions. In one, enter hexo server at the prompt; when prompted, go ahead and browse to the URL provided in the response.

2. The first type of page we'll be adding in is a post – for this, enter hexo new post "Test Post" at the prompt in the second terminal window, and press Enter. You should see an INFO message appear to confirm that Hexo created the page successfully.

3. Go ahead and run the commands shown in Figure 2-3 – if all is well, we should end up with a new page and draft, alongside the post we created in the previous step.

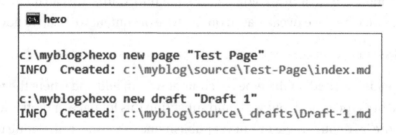

Figure 2-3. *Creating test and draft pages*

4. Next, go ahead and refresh your browser window – you will see the header of each post or page has been created, but not the page or draft. Don't worry. We'll be adding that shortly, but for now, try clicking the header of one of the newly added posts, so you see it in all its glory (Figure 2-4).

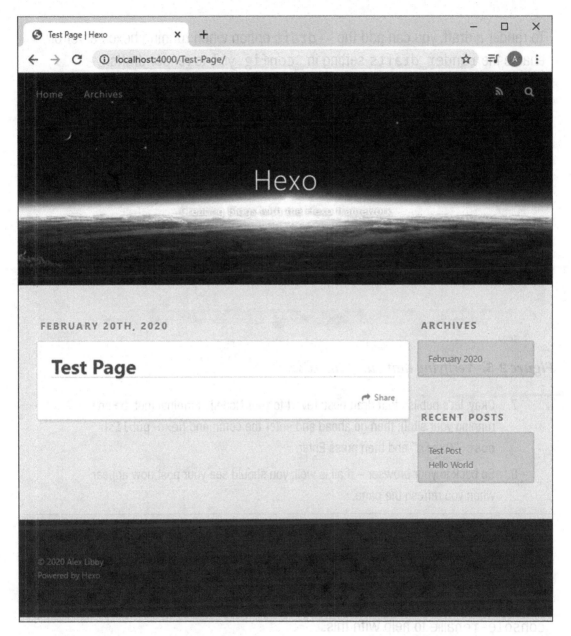

Figure 2-4. Our test page in all its glory

5. To see our new page show, go ahead and enter http://localhost:4000/
    Test-Page/ into your browser address bar and press Enter – you should see
    your page appear, albeit not linked to the main index page (which we will fix
    later in Chapter 3 when we learn about creating and using themes in Hexo).

To render a draft, you can add the `--draft` option when running hexo server or enable the `render_drafts` setting in `_config.yml` to render drafts.

6. To verify our draft page has been created, we have to use a different method – fire up your file manager and browse to the _drafts subfolder in the source folder within your blog. You will see it present, similar to that shown in Figure 2-5.

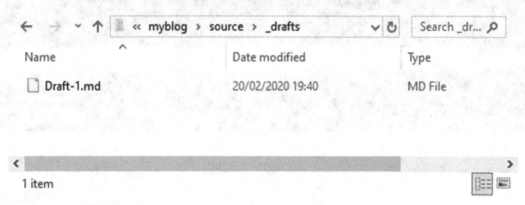

Figure 2-5. *Verifying that our draft exists*

7. Okay, let's publish that draft post: revert to your Node.js terminal (not the one running your site!); then go ahead and enter the command hexo publish post "Draft" and then press Enter.

8. Go back to your browser – if all is well, you should see your post now appear when you refresh the page.

If you take a look at the `source/_drafts` subfolder, you will notice that our draft post is now in the `_posts` folder and a date has also been added to the markdown file to confirm publication. Hexo does not rename drafts as part of the publishing process – you may want to look at `https://github.com/timnew/hexo-console-rename` to help with this.

9. There is one last page type to try out. Crack open a new file in your text editor, and then add in this code at the top:

```
---
title: {{title}}
date: {{date}}
---
```

10. Save the file as book.md in the scaffolds folder, and switch back to your Node. js terminal session (not the one running Hexo, but the other one!). Make sure the working directory is myblog if it isn't already there.

11. At the prompt, enter the following code and press Enter:

```
hexo new book "My Books"
```

12. If all is well, we will get a similar response to previous requests to create posts; go ahead and refresh your browser window, and you should see the new page type appear.

Phew! That was a long exercise! Granted, it seems like a lot of steps to cover, but in reality, you won't need to complete all of them in one go and will only do the steps needed for the type of content you need to add to your blog.

That said, it does cover some important points we need to be aware of, so take a breather, go and grab a drink, and let's work through the changes we made in more detail.

Breaking apart our changes

A blog won't be anything without content – Hexo is certainly no different! As we saw in this exercise, adding posts and pages is a straightforward process – we learned how to achieve this with the hexo new command, for both posts and pages, as well as drafts.

At the same time, we covered off where Hexo stores each type of page in our blog and saw how drafts can be viewed on-screen as a preview but will not be processed until they are fully published.

Further afield, it's important to note that we can override the default behavior used to store pages, using the --path option, thus:

```
hexo new page --path about/me "About me"
```

If we run this command, it will create a source/about/me.md file with the title "About me" set in the front matter section of the post. We must specify a title for each post we create – if we ran a command such as this, it would not result in the behavior you might expect:

```
hexo new page --path about/me
```

It will create a post, which Hexo will store as source/_posts/about/me.md with the title "page" in the front matter; we can only have one argument (page), and the default layout type is post.

Setting the front matter content

When working with Hexo, you will frequently come across this phrase – front matter. What does it mean...?

Well, it's a block of code, either JSON or YAML, that sits at the top of each markdown file; for example, you might see something like this:

```
---
title: Hello Hexo
date: 2020/7/13 19:38:25
---
```

We use it to assign various properties, such as (in this case) a date or title – we might also want to add in other things such as comment tags or categories or perhaps a date when the post was last updated or to override the permalink used for that post. We'll cover how to add in tags and categories in more depth shortly, but for now, a list of available settings is in Table 2-1.

Table 2-1. *A list of page settings*

Setting	Purpose
Layout	The layout of your blog post or page.
Title (posts only)	Title of your blog post (default is the file name).
Date/Updated	The post's published date or last date it was updated – default value is the date of creation or last update, respectively.
Comments	Enables comment feature for the post – the default is true.
Tags/Categories (posts only)	Display either tags or categories (or both) for the post.
Permalink	Overrides the default permalink of the post.
Keywords	The keywords used in meta tags and Open Graph (not recommended).
Excerpt	Adds a page excerpt in plain text to a post or page – Hexo contains a built-in plugin to transform it into a Read More link.

Now that we've set up the basic placeholder pages and posts, our next task is to add in that all-important content – after all, if we want customers to come and visit our blog, we have to give them something worthwhile to read!

To add content, we do this using markdown syntax, much in the same way as we might write posts in GitHub (for those of you who do!). Don't worry if you're not familiar with this. The basic principles of editing are straightforward to get to grips with, as we will see in our next exercise.

Adding text to posts

Okay, now that we know how to add in posts and pages, it's time to flesh them out with some content. The great thing about using markdown is that it is simpler to add in than standard HTML markup; instead, we use a set of symbols to identify when we want to change text, such as altering the size or emboldening content.

There is no better way to learn than to edit content; for our next exercise, we're going to take one of the posts we've created and start to add content in before altering its appearance.

I would recommend having the Markdown Cheat Sheet at `https://www.markdownguide.org/cheat-sheet` open in a separate window, just in case you're not familiar with using Markdown styling!

ADDING TEXT TO POSTS

For this exercise, we'll use the Test Post with Video from the `_posts` subfolder, so make sure you have it open before making these changes:

1. Our first task is to add in content – for this, we need some dummy text. Head over to `https://lipsum.com` and change the number of paragraphs needed to 3. Click Generate Lorem Ipsum; then copy the three paragraphs displayed into the body of the markdown file (below the second set of dashes that close the front matter area).

2. The first change we're going to make is to add in a divider; scroll down to the end of a paragraph, then add in a blank line and then three hyphens, and follow that with a blank line.

3. Next, we 're going to add in an H2 title – after the second blank line from the previous step, add in this line of code:

```
## Displaying videos
```

4. Next, we're going to add in an image caption and center it; scroll down to the image, then leave a blank line, and add in this block (including the blank lines):

```
<center>

##### Cruise boat on river in [Prague](https://www.prague.eu/en).

</center>
```

5. Finally, we're going to add in a code block – we'll use the example of the code added for the image caption. For this, scroll down to the end of the next paragraph, or split an existing one, and add in this text:

```
We added the image using this code:

``##### Cruise boat on river in [Prague](https://www.prague.eu/en).``
```

6. Save the file – if you refresh your browser window and then navigate to the post and click its title, you will see the changes in full display on the screen.

If you would like an example of how markdown should appear, then refer to the `2020-02-22-Test-Post-with-Video.md` example that is in the code download that accompanies this book.

Dissecting the changes made

Although the first step of the last exercise was very easy, adding markdown can trip you up if you're not careful: it's very fussy about spacing!

It might seem like overkill if you're used to writing standard HTML markup; markdown syntax though relies on the correct spacing to interpret where each tag finishes and the next one kicks in.

In this exercise, we worked our way through making some simple changes to our content, by adding in a selection of standard markup tags and reformatting the text to suit. I've chosen a handful of tags (in this case, H2, a horizontal rule, an image caption, and code block), but in reality, I could add in any number of tags – they all follow the same principle of ensuring you allow sufficient space.

If you're not used to writing markup, then I would recommend seeing if your text editor has a markdown syntax plugin; more popular editors such as Visual Studio Code, Atom, or Sublime Text will have something you can plug in to help with formatting or checking syntax.

Adding excerpts

Let's move on. We've started to add in written content to a post. So far, so good, right? What if that happened to be a long post...? Okay, so the content might need to be lengthy, but we don't want it all displayed when viewing the listing pages, right?

That's something we can easily fix by introducing excerpts – this is a typical feature you will see on blogs worldwide. We can provide a little introduction on the summary pages, with a call to action to read more if people want to delve into the detail. Rather than build in something to address this manually, we can make use of a Hexo plugin for this purpose. We're going to use one to add in an excerpt, as part of our next exercise. We'll mark a spot in our markdown with a `<!-- more -->` tag; this will be replaced with a "Read More" link that will open the rest of the article content.

IMPLEMENTING EXCERPTS

To add in an excerpt, follow these steps:

1. First, browse to `https://lipsum.com/` to get some dummy text – when prompted, enter 3 for the number of desired paragraphs, and copy the resulting text.

2. Go ahead and open the `Test-Post.md` file from within the `_posts` subfolder; leave a blank line after the `---`, and then paste in the dummy text.

3. After the first couple of sentences, insert a blank line and then a `<!-- more -->` tag, followed by a second blank line.

4. You should see something akin to the example shown in Figure 2-6.

```
8    - post
9    ---
10
11   Lorem ipsum dolor sit amet, consectet
     venenatis vitae quis nulla.
12
13   <!-- more -->
14
15   Vestibulum quismod justo eget velit v
```

Figure 2-6. *An example of an excerpt in place*

5. Switch back to your browser, and then refresh the page – you should now see a Read More button appear, below the post summary (Figure 2-7).

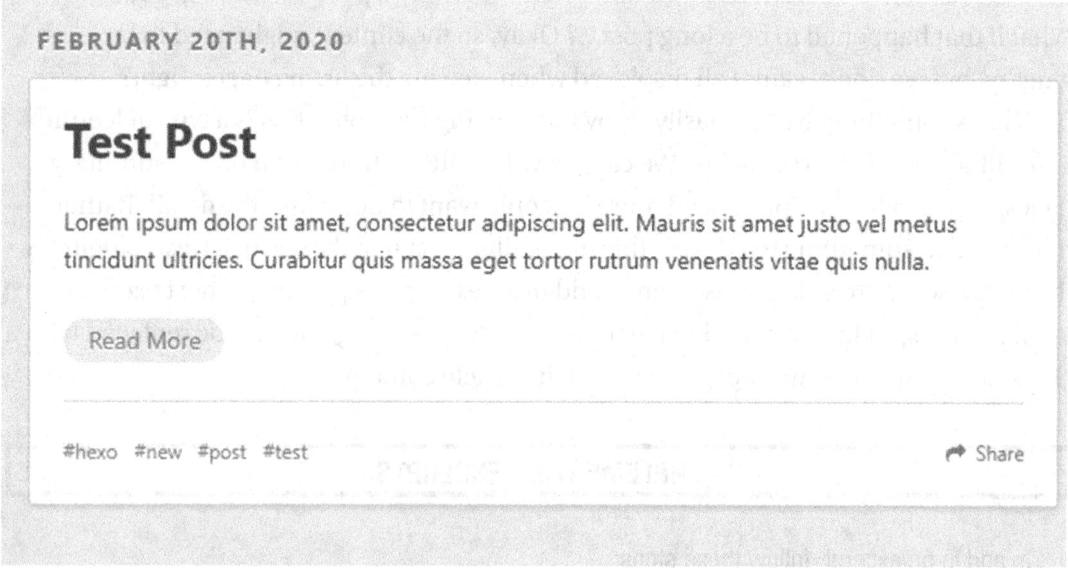

FEBRUARY 20TH, 2020

Test Post

Lorem ipsum dolor sit amet, consectetur adipiscing elit. Mauris sit amet justo vel metus tincidunt ultricies. Curabitur quis massa eget tortor rutrum venenatis vitae quis nulla.

Read More

#hexo #new #post #test   ↱ Share

Figure 2-7. *A Read More link in place*

A nice easy change, but something to consider when adding content – after all, content is king (as people will frequently say). It becomes less regal if you can't provide an upfront summary to entice customers in if you pardon the pun!

Okay, let's change tack. We've added in some content, but it looks rather plain. What about providing something to help make it more interesting visually?

Adding media content

It's time to add in some media, methinks! The simplest we can add in are images; it's time to bring that images folder we talked about back at the start of this chapter as part of our next exercise.

There is, however, something of a little sting in this tail though – images won't display everywhere using a central images folder. To understand why, let's first add in images using this central folder method.

ADDING MEDIA CONTENT

To add in images, work through the following steps – note I've selected an image and based this (and the next) exercise around it. Please adjust to suit if you use a different image:

1. First, we need to create an `images` folder at the top level of our blog (as per the screenshot we saw at the start of this chapter).

2. Go ahead and add in an image into this folder – it's doesn't matter what file format it is, but I would recommend keeping to a medium size. I've used one from the pexels.com site at `https://www.pexels.com/photo/cruise-ship-on-body-of-water-1269805/`; if you want to use it, then I would suggest selecting the small size version.

3. Next, switch to the markdown file marked `test-post.md` that we created earlier – add a blank line after one of the paragraphs, and then add in this line of code:

   `![Cruise boat on river in Prague.](/images/cruiseboat.jpg)`

4. We should have something akin to the screenshot shown in Figure 2-8.

```
     Suspendisse blandit sollicitudin magna at feugiat. Pellentesqu
18
19   ![Cruise boat on river in Prague.](/images/cruiseboat.jpg)
20
21   Ut sagittis libero lorem, in pretium elit dignissim ut. Nulla
```

Figure 2-8. Adding in an image

5. Save the file and close it; then browse to the Test Post blog posting, to see the image appear (Figure 2-9)

condimentum porta interdum. Morbi euismod egestas tincidunt.

Cruise boat on river in Prague.

Figure 2-9. *An image added to our test post using a central folder*

This process looks pretty comprehensive, right? After all, we use standard markdown tags to insert a normal image into a posting – what could go wrong? Well, with Hexo version 3, images won't display at all on the index page, if you use a relative link (but will work fine on the posting page itself).

Using a central folder might not be an issue if you only have a handful of images, but for anything more, this could present a bit of a problem! Don't worry – there is a way around this. Instead of using a central images folder, we can create an images folder on a per-post basis, at the same time as we create the post itself.

Remember how I touched on this subject, near the start of this chapter? Well, the folders that show with the same names as the post files in Figure 2-2 are the folders I'm referring to here; let's dive in and take a look at how this works in more detail.

Improving image coverage

If we find ourselves using more than just a handful of images (and chances are we will), then storing images in a folder next to the post will allow them to be displayed on the index page using relative paths, rather than having to hard-code them!

The change to effect this is very simple – we have to enable the post asset folder setting and then create content as before. This time around, Hexo will create an images folder at the same time. To see how easy this is, let's dive in and take a look at our next exercise.

MAKING IMAGES AVAILABLE EVERYWHERE

To add in images, follow these steps:

1. First, go ahead and stop your blog if it is running – press Ctrl+C in the Node.js terminal window to terminate the Hexo server.

2. Next, crack open the `_config.yml` file in your text editor – look for the `post_asset_folder` and change the value from false to true, as indicated in Figure 2-10.

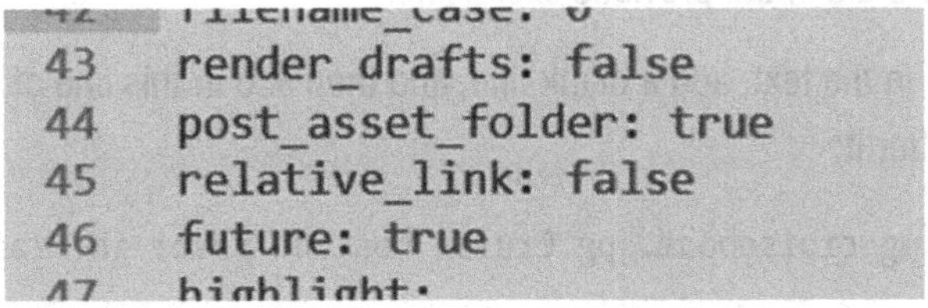

```
42    filename_case: 0
43    render_drafts: false
44    post_asset_folder: true
45    relative_link: false
46    future: true
47    highlight:
```

Figure 2-10. *Updating the post_asset_folder setting*

3. At this point, we can restart the server – in the terminal session, enter hexo `server` and press Enter.

4. If you don't already have two open, fire up a second Node.js terminal session, and then change the working folder to `c:\myblog`.

5. At the prompt, type in hexo `new post "Test Post with Image"` and then press Enter.

6. Once we've created the post, go ahead and find it in the `_posts` folder, as shown in Figure 2-11.

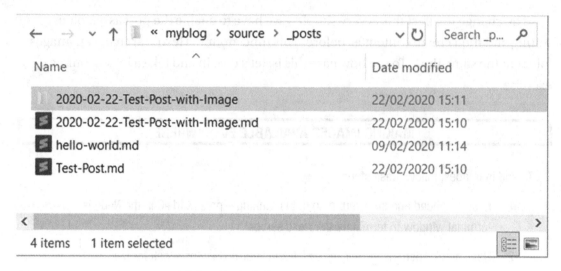

Figure 2-11. *The _posts folder with the newly created images folder*

7. Go ahead and open it – add in some dummy text below the second set of dashes, as we did in the previous exercise.

8. Somewhere in the text, add a blank line, and then add in this line of code and a blank line after it:

    ```
    {% asset_img cruiseboat.jpg Cruise boat on river in Prague %}
    ```

We're effectively doing something similar to the previous exercise, but this time around using a different tactic to pull in the image – have a look at Figure 2-8 from that exercise for a guide.

---

9. Save the file and close it – if you refresh your browser, you will have something similar to Figure 2-12, where we have our image displayed, albeit without a caption.

condimentum porta interdum. Morbi euismod egestas tincidunt.

Cruise boat on river in Prague

Ut sagittis libero lorem, in pretium elit dignissim ut. Nulla sed mattis neque, quis volutpat elit.

Figure 2-12. *Our image displayed using a post images folder*

See how easy that was to make that change? Granted, we have images stored in multiple locations, but at least we will be able to display content correctly! There are a couple of points of note when inserting images, so let's take a breather and review the changes in more detail.

Breaking apart the changes

Adding images is an essential part of creating blog content – some people may like the minimalist theme on blogs that contain just text, but that's not for everyone!

We kicked off by adding an image using the standard markdown format for images; we saw how easy this was to display images, but also learned that this wouldn't work for certain page types. We then adapted our approach by first enabling the post asset folder switch, before creating a new post that automatically creates a media folder at the same time.

We then took the same markdown we used in the first example, before adapting it to use the `asset_img` tag to reference the image from the post images folder, not the central images folder created at the beginning of the first exercise.

Okay, let's move on. Adding in static images is a good start, but people expect more: how about including media such as videos and even sound? Adding media adds a whole new dimension to the content and can make it easier to impart information. Let's take a look at a couple of examples in more detail.

Linking to external content

So far, we've created pages and posts and added text and images – our blog is beginning to take shape. However, there is one thing missing – what about more interesting material, such as videos or even sound?

I've seen hundreds of blogs over the years, and frequently find ones with at least one video present – this has become the de facto way to help express content that would otherwise be difficult to impart in textual format.

Thankfully, adding media is easy with Hexo. For this, we need to make use of two plugins – `https://github.com/tea3/hexo-tag-soundcloud` (for SoundCloud, naturally!) and `https://github.com/m80126colin/hexo-tag-owl` for other media formats such as YouTube or Vimeo.

We have a little work to do to set them up, so without further ado, let's take a look at the steps required to display videos and sound in our blog posts and pages.

ADDING EXTERNAL CONTENT

To add in media from external sources, such as YouTube or SoundCloud, follow these steps:

1. We'll start with YouTube – for this, we'll use a plugin to import YouTube videos. Fire up a Node.js command prompt if you don't already have a spare one open, and then make sure the working folder is `c:\myblog`.

2. At the prompt, enter `npm install hexo-tag-owl –save`; then press Enter.

3. Once done, enter this command at the prompt and press Enter to create a new post:

   `hexo new post "Test Post with YouTube"`

4. Next, crack open the `Test-Post-with-YouTube.md` file, and add in some dummy text – for convenience, go ahead and copy text from one of the earlier post files, but make sure you add it in **below** the second set of dashes.

5. Some way down the file, and in between two paragraphs, add a blank line and then this line of code, and follow it with a blank line:

```
{% owl youtube aqz-KE-bpKQwith  %}
```

6. Save the file and close it. Go ahead and refresh your browser window; you should see the post summary present. Click the title to go to the full version – if all is well, you will see a video appear (Figure 2-13).

Ut sagittis libero lorem, in pretium elit dignissim ut. N

Figure 2-13. *A post with a YouTube video displayed*

We now have a video displayed – we will work on resizing it when we cover styling in the next chapter.

Let's crack on with part 2 of this demo, where we will add in something similar to display music from SoundCloud:

1. First, switch back to the Node.js terminal session that is running your Hexo server, and then press `Ctrl+C` to stop it.

2. As before, we need to install a plugin to display music from SoundCloud – for this, we will use the `hexo-tag-SoundCloud` plugin. Fire up a Node.js terminal session and then enter this at the prompt and press Enter:

```
npm install hexo-tag-soundcloud --save
```

3. Once completed, enter this command and press Enter:

    ```
    hexo new post "Test Post for SoundCloud"
    ```

    Keep the session open – we will need it shortly.

4. We now need to add some content – for this, open up the `Test-Post-for-SoundCloud.md` file from within the `_posts` subfolder under the source folder.

5. Grab a copy of the dummy text we've used in a previous post – ideally, one that has had an image in it, as we will replace that with a link to the SoundCloud player. Paste this into the open file, save it, and close the file.

6. Next, go ahead and open the `_config.yml` file at the root of the `myblog` folder, then scroll to the bottom, and leave a blank line before adding in this code:

    ```
    #Soundcloud settings
    soundcloud:
      height: 100
      visual: false
    ```

7. Go ahead and save the file and then close it – revert to your Node.js terminal session that had the Hexo server running, then enter `hexo server` at the prompt, and press Enter.

8. Now refresh your browser window – if all is well, we should see our new SoundCloud post appear. Click the title to view the post and see our SoundCloud player in all its glory (Figure 2-14).

Figure 2-14. *Our post with a SoundCloud player present*

Okay, I must admit that these two last exercises might reveal something of my tastes – at least musically! But, in all seriousness, it doesn't matter what the content is, as it will be a similar process for setting up the blog to support that content.

In this last exercise, we ran through the steps to introduce two different types of content; let's take a moment to review the changes in more detail and why it's important to plan which plugins we use when configuring our blogs.

Breaking apart the code

We've seen just now how easy it is to add in images – it's an essential part of creating blog content, particularly if we want to attract and keep readers visiting our site! Adding images is just a start, though: to give our content that all-important edge, adding videos (and, to a lesser extent, sound) is a must.

To do so in a Hexo blog requires a few more steps, as we saw from our previous exercise. We started by installing the `hexo-tag-owl` plugin, to give us support for incorporating videos (in this case, YouTube ones). We then created a new post to show off our video – in much the same way as we did with images, we dropped in a tag to tell our post to include a video, along with the ID of the video.

Adding sound worked in much the same manner, but required a couple of extra steps: we added in some settings for SoundCloud into our `_config.yml` file. This change switches the player into a compact, nonvisual mode and sets the size it should display at on-screen.

The key takeaway from this exercise, though, isn't just the installation of plugins; we need to plan how our content should be displayed. It's important to do this, so that we only use the plugins that are needed and do not include unnecessary content that serves no purpose within our blog configuration.

Okay, let's move on. Thus far, we've made all of our changes using a text editor. Nothing technically wrong with this approach, but it's not the world's easiest! No problem – we can fix that. Some kind soul has developed a Hexo plugin that allows us to run up a GUI-based interface that makes editing files so much easier. It's pretty easy to set up, so let's check it out in more detail.

Managing content

Once our blog is in production use, we don't want to be spending time editing content in a text editor – not only is it awkward but it also opens up the risk that we inadvertently edit the wrong file!

To get around this, we can set up an admin portal that allows us to focus on writing and managing posts and pages without having to worry about inadvertently editing files that could break your blog. The plugin is available on GitHub at `https://github.com/geekwen/hexo-local-admin`; we can install using the standard method for installing Hexo plugins.

SETTING UP OUR ADMIN PORTAL

Setting up the admin portal is straightforward – to do so, follow these steps:

1. First, we need to stop our Hexo blog – for that, revert to the Node.js terminal session that is running the Hexo server, and press `Ctrl+C` to stop it.

2. Once done, enter this command at the prompt and then press Enter:

   ```
   npm install -g hexo-local-admin
   ```

3. NPM will go away and install our plugin – when done, enter this command and press Enter to set up the admin portal:

   ```
   hexo-admin -h
   ```

4. It will prompt for the blog's location (-r switch) and theme (-t switch) in use – for this, enter this command and press Enter:

   ```
   hexo-admin -r c:\myblog -t landscape
   ```

5. If all is good, we should be able to start the portal – to do that, enter `hexo-admin start` at the prompt and press Enter.

6. We will then see our admin portal appear if we navigate to `http://localhost:4001`, as indicated in Figure 2-15, shown overleaf.

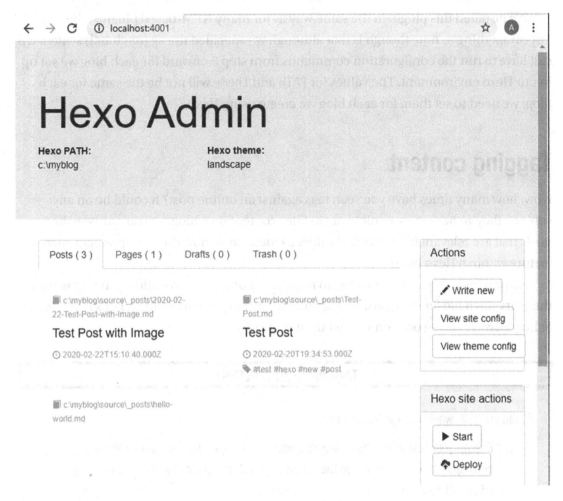

Figure 2-15. *Our newly installed admin portal*

Hopefully, this will make your lives a little easier when it comes to editing content! Have a browse around – it should be fairly self-explanatory as to what each button does. That aside, there are a couple of things to note about how we installed this plugin, so while it's still fresh, let's cover these off in more detail.

Breaking apart our code

One of the great features about Hexo is that many of the features we can use are not all part of the core framework – hexo-admin is one such tool that was written by a third party but is nevertheless one that should be part of your Hexo development environment.

We installed this plugin in the same way as for many NPM-based plugins; the important thing to note though is that although we specified the -g (or global) switch, we still have to run the configuration commands from step 3 onward for each blog we set up in our Hexo environment. The values for PATH and theme will not be the same for each blog; we need to set them for each blog we create using Hexo.

Tagging content

Now, how many times have you seen tags against an online post? It could be on any subject; they're perfect as a quick way to filter content on a blog, so you only see those posts that are relevant to your target subject. Question is: how do we implement such a feature within a Hexo blog?

No problem – it's an easy change to make. In short, it involves adding in tags within the markdown file for each post or page that we want to tag in our blog. Let's take a look at how easy it is to tag our content in our next exercise.

TAGGING OUR CONTENT

To tag content, work through these steps:

1. Fire up your text editor, then navigate your way to open the markdown file that corresponds to your post – in this example, I will use one called `Test-Post-with-Video.md`.

2. By default, the tags entry will be blank – go ahead and add in some tags, similar to the ones highlighted in this code example:

```
---
title: Test Post 2
date: 2020-02-20 20:02:15
tags:
- test
- hexo
- new
- post
---
```

3. Save the file – the tags will automatically appear at the bottom of your chosen post (Figure 2-16) when refreshing the browser window and clicking the post summary to see the post in full.

placerat metus.

#hexo #media #test #youtube

Figure 2-16. *Our chosen tags added to a post*

4. We can add categories in the same way, although there is a little more to it – for this, add in the word categories, immediately before the closing - - -, followed by the categories as listed in this example.

```
[Sports, Baseball]
[MLB, American League, Boston Red Sox]
[MLB, American League, New York Yankees]
Rivalries
```

5. Save the file – if all is well, we will see this listing on the right, once we've refreshed our browser window page (Figure 2-17).

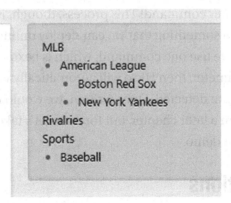

MLB
* American League
  * Boston Red Sox
  * New York Yankees
Rivalries
Sports
* Baseball

Figure 2-17. *A list of categories added to a post*

If you take a closer look at the top of the page that uses categories, you may see the categories list appear again; it's easy to remove! We'll see how when we take a more in-depth look at themes in Chapter 3.

See how easy that was? It's a common feature seen across thousands of blogs, and well-chosen tags will be a real time-saver for viewers when it comes to searching for relevant content within your blog.

Okay, let's change tack. We've been through all of the basic tasks we can perform to generate and arrange our content; it's time to see what the final article looks like in all its glory! Yes, it's time to process and publish our content, so let's take a look at the steps involved in getting your content into a format that is ready to view ahead of releasing it to the world at large.

Processing and previewing content

We're almost at the end of creating our example pages, but there is one more task we need to perform – processing our files, ready for preview, and eventual deployment online.

It might sound like a complex process, but it is far from the truth – indeed, the core part of this is just a one-liner command! This process, though, is essential to transform all of our markup files into something that we can deploy online as our finished site.

To perform this task, we use one command, which is `hexo generate` – if we supply the optional --watch parameter, then Hexo will automatically watch for any changes and write new versions if any are detected. Once written, we would then deploy them; this is something we will cover in a later chapter, but for now, let's take a look at the generation process as part of our next demo.

Making assumptions

To give you a flavor of what our completed demo will look like, Figure 2-18 shows what it will look like when running in my preconfigured local web server (and away from our blog development area).

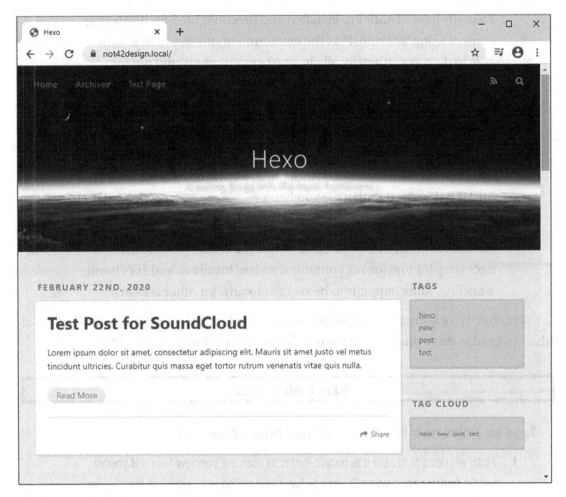

Figure 2-18. *A preview of our completed blog*

Before we get into the detail of our next exercise though, there are a couple of things we need to be aware of:

- For this next exercise, I will assume you have a local web server (such as Apache) set up; it doesn't need to have any databases or ancillary features such as PHP installed.

I already have MAMP Pro installed and preconfigured for displaying content using "localhost" as the environment; the key here is to be able to display content locally in a test environment, and not for public access.

- The steps I provide will be a guideline to how we process the files – many of the steps will depend on whether you use web space or localhost and, if it is the latter, which web server you use. I would recommend the latter option, though, as we will cover deployment to the Web in more detail in a later chapter.

- The screenshot at the end of this next exercise will show our preview files under an HTTPS-secured area. Using a secure website isn't necessary for previewing content; standard localhost and HTTP will work fine. Mine happens to be secure already, for other reasons!

Now that we've seen a preview of how our finished article will look, let's take a look at what we need to do to prepare our content for previewing locally on our PCs.

PREPARING CONTENT

To get our content ready for putting online, work through these steps:

1. First, we need to create a separate folder to host our preview files – if you've set up Apache, then you will already have one called www, which is fine for our needs.

2. Next, fire up a Node.js terminal session, and then change the working folder to c:\myblog.

3. At the prompt, enter this command, and press Enter:

   ```
   hexo clean && hexo generate
   ```

4. Once done, copy the contents of the public folder from within the myblog folder to your preview folder.

5. We can now preview the results; make sure your local web server is running, and then browse to http://localhost/ to view your content, which will look similar to the screenshot at the start of this exercise.

We now have a blog that is operational and beginning to take shape! Of course, this is just a preview, but it will give you a flavor of how it will look when we release it into production. We've covered a useful technique here, which you will no doubt need to use on multiple occasions when using Hexo. Let's take a look at what `hexo clean && generate` does in more detail.

Breaking apart the changes

Although we've made a few assumptions about how we're hosting our content (for now), the key to this last exercise was the `hexo clean && hexo generate` commands. What do these two commands achieve, and why is it important to run them?

They are needed to process all of your markdown files and transform them into a set of static files ready for deploying to your final host. To a certain extent, this happens when you run `hexo server`, but it's an inefficient way of doing things; we run `hexo clean && hexo generate` to create the final version of your latest content.

The first command, `hexo clean`, wipes the content from the public folder at the top of our blog; this is where Hexo creates our static content using `hexo generate`, ready for deployment.

"But there's more…"

Yes, indeed there is – the generate command comes with a couple of switches. We can add `--watch` to automatically generate content if it has been changed (via a check on the SHA1 checksum value) and `--deploy`, which will push changes up to our final web server.

Also, it's worth noting that we have a couple of options we can use if we **don't** want to transform content. The first, `skip_render`, is an option we can use our `_config.yml` file, thus:

```
skip_render: "mypage/**/*"
```

Changing this setting to true will process files such as `source/mypage/index.html` and `source/mypage/code.js`, but won't alter them. We can use the same approach when processing posts – this will exclude a post with the `filename test-post.md`:

```
skip_render: "_posts/test-post.md"
```

The second is `layout: false` – this can be specified as a tag within the front matter section of any markdown file, as indicated in Figure 2-19.

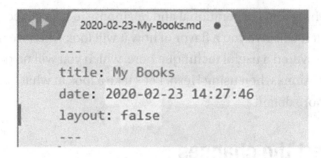

Figure 2-19. *A post with layout: false set*

If we wanted to push things even further, then we could look at putting these commands into a Node.js script, but that would be something for another time!

We'll talk about deployment in more detail in Chapter 6.

Summary

Our journey through the world that is Hexo is only just starting – so far, we've built a basic blog and learned how to start populating it with content using Markdown syntax. We've covered some useful tips in this respect, over the course of this chapter; let's take a moment to review what we have learned.

We started by exploring how Hexo stores content – this covered the different types and where we can find them within our blog project folder. We then moved onto creating different types of pages or posts, before starting to add text and markdown tags to a post.

Next up, we started to look at how to fine-tune or add visual interest to our content – this included adding an excerpt and tags, as well as learning how to add videos, media, and the like. At the same time, we covered off a useful trick to help manage content through a GUI-based admin client that can be installed for each blog we create.

We then rounded out the chapter by understanding the steps required to generate a cut of the content as static files, before viewing them in a local environment (and which would allow us to check the content).

We've certainly covered a lot of material, but our journey doesn't stop there – things are going to get interesting! The next stop is to start updating our theme; the landscape one we're using is very functional, but could definitely be improved! Stay with me, as I will reveal how, in the next chapter.

CHAPTER 3

Creating Themes

By now, we've started to add in some test posts, along with media and videos. Our blog has limited content in it, but what about the look and feel of our content? We're not limited to the landscape theme that is enabled by default, right?

Absolutely not – welcome to the world of themes in Hexo! There are dozens of themes available from the main Hexo website: you can see the list at `https://hexo.io/themes`. The use of an existing theme is just a starting point, though – if we're not happy with what's available, then as Hexo uses JavaScript, standard HTML, and CSS, it's a cinch to start designing themes.

Creating a theme can open up a world of possibilities – throughout this chapter and the next, I'll take you on a whistle-stop tour through how to create a simple theme that you can use to develop for your own needs. We'll start with setting up the framework and navigation in this chapter, before switching to adding in widgets, comments, and more in Chapter 4. At the same time, we'll also take a look at how we might publish them for others to use (yikes – yes, your work can be made public!), but before we do so, let's begin by seeing how we change to a different theme.

Changing themes

I'm sure someone once said, "We have to start somewhere" – there is no better place than to learn how to adapt to one of the dozens of themes already available for Hexo.

You can see many of them listed on the themes page on the Hexo site; I've elected to use the Daily theme (from `https://github.com/GallenHu/hexo-theme-Daily`) as the basis for our next exercise, but you can equally use any theme from the Hexo site at `https://hexo.io/themes/`.

© Alex Libby 2020
A. Libby, *Practical Hexo*, https://doi.org/10.1007/978-1-4842-6089-0_3

Although the core install process is the same for all themes, you will come across instances where you might need to install extra plugins. It's a good idea to check the GitHub page for the theme to be sure you don't miss anything!

To give you a flavor of how our site will look once we've installed the new theme, Figure 3-1 shows a screenshot with the Daily theme activated.

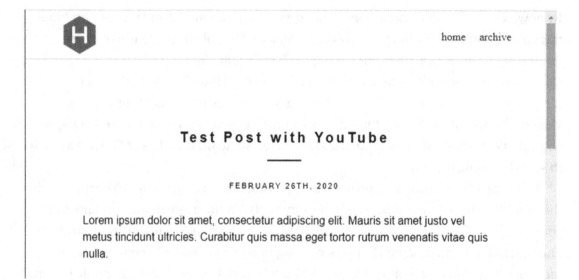

Figure 3-1. *Our site with the updated theme now installed*

With this in mind, let's crack on and take a look at the steps to change themes in more detail.

SWITCHING THEMES

To change the theme in use, use these steps – this change requires stopping the Hexo server, so make sure you've done this before continuing:

1. First, fire up a Node.js terminal session, and then change the working folder to our myblog project folder.

2. At the prompt, enter this command and press Enter: git clone https://github.com/GallenHu/hexo-theme-Daily.gitthemes/Daily.

3. Git will download the theme and unpack it into the themes/Daily folder. Once finished, you will see confirmation, similar to that shown in Figure 3-2.

```
c:\myblog>git clone https://github.com/GallenHu/hexo-theme-Daily.git themes/Daily
Cloning into 'themes/Daily'...
remote: Enumerating objects: 3, done.
remote: Counting objects: 100% (3/3), done.
remote: Compressing objects: 100% (3/3), done.
remote: Total 439 (delta 0), reused 0 (delta 0), pack-reused 436 eceiving objects:  98% (4:
Receiving objects:  99% (435/439)
Receiving objects: 100% (439/439), 225.74 KiB | 1.20 MiB/s, done.
Resolving deltas: 100% (218/218), done.
```

Figure 3-2. *Cloning the Daily theme to our local blog*

4. For this particular theme, we have to install an additional plugin – hexo-renderer-sass. This plugin uses the Sass preprocessor library for managing and applying styles; don't worry too much about how it works – suffice to say it will process Sass rules into valid CSS as part of installing the theme.

If you would like to learn more about Sass, then please check out my book *Introducing Dart Sass*, published by Apress.

---

5. Go ahead and fire up your text editor, then crack open the _config.yml file located at the root of your blog folder, and scroll down to the theme: entry.

6. Go ahead and change the word landscape to daily – you should now have something akin to Figure 3-3.

```
93    # Extensions
94    ## Plugins: https://hexo.io/plugins/
95    ## Themes: https://hexo.io/themes/
96    theme: daily
97
```

Figure 3-3. *Changing the installed theme*

7. Save the file, and then close it – switch back to your Node.js terminal window. At the prompt, enter hexo server -no-optional and press Enter – if you then refresh your browser, you should see the new theme in operation, as shown at the start of this exercise.

We now have a new theme in place – this might suit some, but if you're like me, finding something that ticks all of your boxes on your checklist will be difficult, if not impossible!

What if we could create something that suits our needs? Well, as we are about to find out, it's straightforward to do: Hexo themes are just a mix of CSS and EJS (or Extended JavaScript) files, stored in a particular folder structure. Let's dive in and take a look at what such a structure looks like in practice.

Exploring theme file structure

When you begin to develop themes for Hexo, it's essential to be familiar with how they are structured; as with many blogging systems, it's not a case of being just one file in a single folder!

For this chapter, we're going to develop a simple theme for Hexo called Coffee (being a developer, it's no surprise why I chose that name!). I will take you through the different elements that make up a theme and how they all fit in together. We've already seen how to add such a theme to our blog. Without further ado, let's dive in and take a look at the innards of what will become our theme.

A Hexo theme is made up of a mix of files and folders, all stored within a single folder that takes the theme name and is in the themes folder at the root of our blog folder. You can see the start of this in Figure 3-4, for our sample Coffee theme.

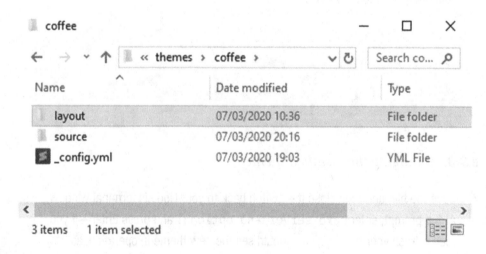

Figure 3-4. *Our basic theme structure*

The layout folder stores the individual template files that make up the theme – our sample theme will contain three core files, as listed in Table 3-1.

Table 3-1. *The file structure of a Hexo theme*

File name	Purpose
index.ejs	To construct a list of posts and their summaries as an index on the main page.
layout.ejs	To define the markup used for the page structure, such as header, sidebar, and footer.
post.ejs	To build the content and layout for each post.

Also, we have a _partial folder – this stores templates for individual elements, such as the header, menu, and sidebar. We also have a _widget folder, which holds the various widgets you will typically see in the sidebar of a blog.

Don't worry too much about how this works as we will cover it all in detail in this chapter; it's enough to know that these files use the same format as the main ones and that Hexo imports them during generation.

Okay, enough digging around files. Let's crack on and develop our theme! For this, we will, of course, need our usual text editor; I would recommend finding and installing a syntax file for Extended JavaScript as well, as this will help with reading the code. Most well-known editors that support syntax files will likely have something suitable that you can download and install for your editor.

Creating our first theme

Coffee – the godsend of any developer. Late nights and the need to get something finished are I am sure somethings with which many of you will be familiar! It is indeed perhaps no surprise why I've chosen this as the name for the theme we're going to develop – and no, it's not to encourage us to drink that beverage to excess!

But I digress. For the next few pages, we will start with building the folder structure for our theme, before fleshing it out with the individual page and widgets and finally adding styles. Let's begin with a look at the folder and configuration file structure needed for our theme.

```
                   CREATING OUR THEME STRUCTURE
```

To set up the basic structure for our theme, go ahead with these steps – make sure the Hexo
server is not running first:

1. The first step is to create our theme folder – navigate to the `themes` folder in
   your blog folder, and create a new folder inside it called `coffee`.

2. Next, we need to create a `_config.yml` file – crack open your text editor, and
   add the following code to a new file, saving it at the root of your blog folder:

   ```
   # Header
   menu:
     Home: /
     Archives: /archives
     Test Page: /Test-page/
     Test Post with YouTube: /uncategorized/Test-Post-with-YouTube/

   # Read More text
   excerpt_link: ...continue reading
   ```

3. Inside the coffee folder, go ahead and create two new folders – `source` and
   `layout`. For help on what it should look like, take a look back at Figure 3-4 for
   a guide.

4. Once created, navigate into the source folder and create a new folder called
   `css`.

5. Navigate back up a level and then into the layout folder – this time, create a
   folder called `_partial`.

At this stage, we now have a theme structure in place – we can now use this to start
adding in the various template elements that will make up our theme.

It's worth noting that we might add other files and folders to help develop our theme;
for now, we've focused on the core elements needed to operate our theme. There are
a couple of important points we should cover off as part of this demo, so let's take a
moment to review the changes made in more detail.

Breaking apart the changes

If you've spent any time working with blogging frameworks such as WordPress, then you will be familiar with the need to set up a suitable folder structure for each theme we create. The names and exact content will differ, but the principle is still the same – it's no different with Hexo.

In this instance, we created several folders to store content, using a recognized structure that allows Hexo to import each when it generates our final HTML content. The only point of note here, though, is the creation of a second `_config.yml` file. "Another one?" I hear you ask. Yes, we do need to have a second; this controls the content within the theme **and not the site as a whole**.

Inside it, we've added the basic terms that we will use for our menu navigation (see later in this chapter), as well as defining what we will use as a Read More link text. We've also incorporated Bootstrap into our theme – this we use to style text and some of the buttons.

I'm personally not a fan of Bootstrap, as I think it is often misused; we'll talk more about its use later in the chapter when we cover the next steps for future development.

Okay, let's crack on. We've set up our folder structure, so the next stage is to add in the all-important files that make up our theme. We will run this as a two-stage exercise; you may want to get a drink and pause for a moment before we make a start.

Constructing theme files

With our theme folder structure and `_config.yml` file now in place, we can begin to make progress on creating our theme.

The next stage is to start adding in the relevant page types that make up our theme; this will be a two-stage exercise. We'll begin with setting up the core files, before moving on to fine-tuning the experience in the second part of our demo.

ADDING THEME FILES: PART 1

To start creating our theme files, work through these steps – make sure you've stopped any existing instance of the Hexo server, before continuing:

1. First, we need to extract three files from the code download that accompanies this book; go ahead and save copies of `index.ejs`, `layout.ejs`, and `post.ejs` into the `layouts` subfolder.

2. We need an image for our header, so go ahead and choose one. There are dozens of free picture libraries available online if you don't have one; my personal favorite is pexels.com. I will use the image at `https://www.pexels.com/photo/white-ceramic-mug-filled-with-coffee-beside-coffee-beans-678654/`.

3. Next, we need to create three additional files – for this, crack open your text editor, and add the following code to a new file:

```
<div class="blog-masthead">
  <div class="container">
    <nav class="blog-nav">
      <% for (var i in theme.menu){ %>
        <a class="blog-nav-item" href="<%- url_for(theme.menu[i])
        %>"><%= i %></a>
      <% } %>
    </nav>
  </div>
</div>
```

4. Save this as `_menu.ejs` in the `_partial` folder. Next, add this code to a new file, and save it as `_header.ejs` in the same location:

```
<div class='row text-center'>
  <h1 class="blog-title"><%= config.title %></h1>
  <p class="lead blog-description">
    <% if (config.subtitle){ %>
      <%= config.subtitle %><% } %>
    </p>
</div>
```

5. We have one more to do – go ahead and add the following code to a new file, saving it as _sidebar.ejs, again in the same location as before:

```
<% for(var widget in theme.widgets){ %>
  <%- partial('_widget/' + widget) %>
<% }; %>
```

6. We can now generate the HTML – fire up a Node.js terminal session, and then change the working folder to c:\myblog.

7. At the prompt, enter this command and press Enter – this will remove any existing theme files and generate a fresh copy of our theme and content:

```
hexo clean && hexo generate
```

8. Once done, enter hexo server -no-optional at the prompt and press Enter – when prompted, browse to http://localhost:4000, and you should see our theme displayed, similar to that shown in Figure 3-5.

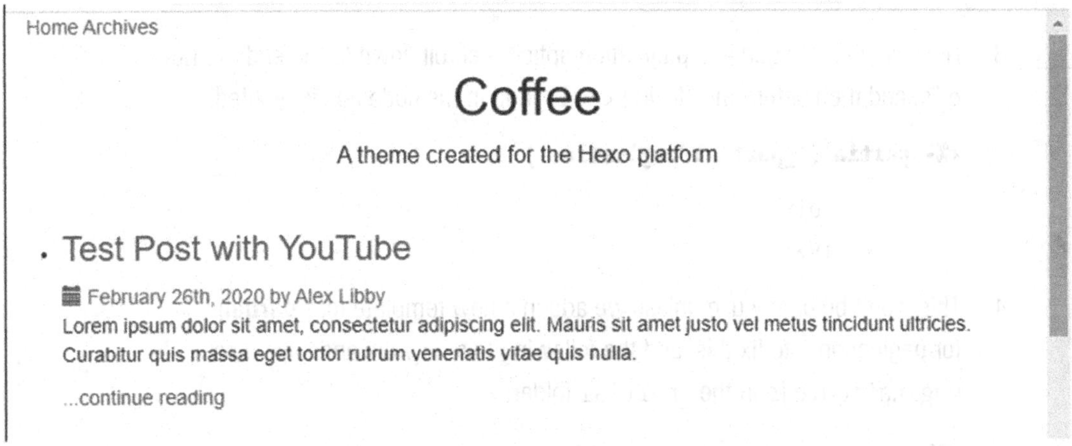

Home Archives

Coffee

A theme created for the Hexo platform

. Test Post with YouTube

February 26th, 2020 by Alex Libby
Lorem ipsum dolor sit amet, consectetur adipiscing elit. Mauris sit amet justo vel metus tincidunt ultricies. Curabitur quis massa eget tortor rutrum venenatis vitae quis nulla.

...continue reading

Figure 3-5. *Our basic theme in place, without styling*

Our (unstyled) theme is now in place – granted, it won't win any style awards, but at least our content is now displayed!

Setting up the content is just the first part, though; there are more changes we will be making to build out functionality within our theme. We still have plenty more to do, so get a drink and take a breather for a moment; when you're ready, let's continue with the second part of this exercise.

ADDING THEME FILES: PART 2

In the second part of our demo, we're going to tweak some of the functionality and add in some new features; to do this, stop the Hexo server and then follow these steps:

1. The first change we will make is to add in a blog post excerpt feature – for this, crack open `index.ejs` from the root of our theme folder, and look for `<div class=" text-muted">`.

2. Follow this down to the closing `</div>` (on or around line 16). Leave a blank line, and then add in this code:

```
<% if(post.excerpt) { %>
  <%= post.excerpt %>

  <a href="<%- config.root %><%- post.path %>">
  <%- theme.excerpt_link %>
  </a>
<% } %>
```

3. Next, we want to add in a pagination option – scroll down to the end of `index.ejs`, and then before the closing `</ul>`, add in the code as highlighted:

```
<%- partial('_partial/pagination') %>

        </ul>
      </div>
```

4. This won't be of any use unless we add in a new template (or **_partial**) for pagination – to fix this, add the following to a new file and save it as `pagination.ejs` in the `_partial` folder:

```
<nav>
  <ul class="pager">
    <% if (page.prev){ %>
      <li><a href="<%- config.root %><%- page.prev_link %>">Previous</a></li>
    <% } %>
    <% if (page.next){ %>
      <li><a href="<%- config.root %><%- page.next_link %>">Next</a></li>
    <% } %>
  </ul>
</nav>
```

5. We also need to update the main _config.yml file (not the one in the theme folder!) – crack that file open in your editor, and look for the per_page setting. Change this to 5 for now – this is to test pagination works correctly. In production, this would be better at 10:

```
_config.yml:
index_generator:
  path: ''
  per_page: 5
  order_by: -date
```

6. The next change is to add in the author's name for each post, which we need to do in two locations: post.ejs and index.ejs. Open each in turn, and then alter the code as highlighted:

```
<%= date(page.date, config.date_format) %>
<% if(page.author) { %>
  by <%- page.author %>
<% } %>
```

7. We're making good progress. There is however one more change left to make. The next one is to display the tags and categories assigned to each post. For this, open post.ejs (in the layout folder), and add in the following code immediately after this line: <%- page.content %> and before the closing </div>:

```
<%- partial('_partial/article-tags', {item: page}) %>
<%- partial('_partial/article-categories', {item: page}) %>
```

Make sure you add in some categories and tags – for a reminder how, refer back to Chapter 2.

---

8. At this point, go ahead and save all of your changes. Fire up (or revert to) a Node.js terminal session and enter hexo clean && hexo generate new files based on your new theme.

9. Once done, enter hexo server -no-optional to restart the server; you can now browse to your blog at http://localhost:4000/. It will look similar to the screenshot shown at the end of the previous exercise, but this time with new features added to your blog.

Wow! That was a hefty couple of exercises! Well done if you managed to get to the end; it seems like a lot of changes, but they are ones that you will need to make when creating and tweaking your new theme. We've covered a lot of changes in the last two exercises, so let's pause for a moment to review these changes in more detail.

Understanding what happened

Creating a theme can be very rewarding – it may feel like a lot of changes need to be made, but seeing the result come together far outweighs any pain you see during development. We've spent some time adding in the core files and functionality that make up our theme, so let's take a moment to review the changes made in the previous two exercises.

We kicked off by setting up the basic folder structure, including the creation of our theme's `_config.yml` file. We then moved onto setting up copies of the three core files for our theme, before downloading (or sourcing) a suitable header image for our site. We then worked our way through creating our `_menu.ejs`, `_header.ejs,` and `_sidebar.ejs` files that form ancillary parts of our theme. With the content and structure in place, we then turned our attention to compiling the code into static HTML files before restarting our server and previewing the results of our work in a browser.

Assuming that you saw our blog appear, then you might think the next stage is to style it, right? Unfortunately, not – we still have more to add! Yes, indeed, we do – for example, we don't have a comments feature, and we're missing some of the widgets you might typically see on blog sites. Fret not – we're going to cover all of these and more in detail, but before we do, there is one topic we need to cover off, which is the subject of variables.

Using variables in Hexo

As we've already seen, Hexo uses JavaScript – it means we can make use of standard JavaScript constructs in our code. One that is of particular interest is variables; take, for example, this extract of code from the `article-tags.ejs` file:

```
<% if (page.tags && page.tags.length){ %>
<%
  var tags = [];
```

```
page.tags.forEach(function(tag){
  tags.push('<a href="' + config.root + tag.path + '">#' + tag.name + '</a>');
});
%>
```

See how some of the tags in this example have been highlighted? These are unique to Hexo and allow us to access parts of the Hexo configuration (and content) others can't – okay, yes, that was a slight take on a well-known Danish beer advertisement, for those who recognize the analogy!

These are useful variables to master in Hexo – in a nutshell, we use them as objects to reference individual Hexo elements. We list the important ones in Table 3-2.

Table 3-2. *Key variables in Hexo*

Page type	Purpose
Site	An object reference to site-wide information, such as `site.posts` (used to reference all posts in a blog). Great for displaying statistics in a widget!
Page	A reference to information on the current page for a post, such as the title and date. The exact content depends on the type of page, such as post, index, or page.
Config	A JavaScript representation of all settings stored in the main `_config.yml` belonging to a blog.
Theme	An object representation of the theme's `_config.yml` file.

You can view the full list of variables at `https://hexo.io/docs/variables.html`.

Okay, let's move on. We've added in content, media, and several widgets. Our blog is starting to take shape now, but there is one key element missing – what about navigating around the site? We've alluded to it briefly with the tags added in the first part of this section; is there anything else left to do?

Adding navigation

Up until now, we've added in several example pages (and posts). This is great, but one question remains: how on earth are we to navigate to them? It's all very well adding in pages and posts, but it makes it very hard to view content if we can't get to them...!

Fortunately, this is easy to fix – we can make use of data files in Hexo. Introduced in version 3, this allows us to store content not already available in templates or posts, or which we might want to reuse somewhere else in our blog, in JSON or YAML files within the _data subfolder within the source folder of our blog. We then use a little script to pull this file in and iterate through any entries contained within each file. As our menu structure is straightforward, we'll keep it in the main _config.yml file for now, but I will go through how to store it separately at the end of the next exercise.

No matter where the content is stored, it produces static links akin to those shown in the example in Figure 3-6, once we've processed our menu content.

```
▼<div id="header-inner" class="inner">
  ▼<nav id="main-nav">
    ▶<a id="main-nav-toggle" class="nav-icon">…</a>
     <a class="main-nav-link" href="/">Home</a>
     <a class="main-nav-link" href="/archives">Archives</a>
     <a class="main-nav-link" href="/Test-page/"> Test Page </a>
     <a class="main-nav-link" href="/uncategorized/Test-Post-with-YouTube/"> Test
     Post with YouTube </a>
  </nav>
```

Figure 3-6. *Example navigation links generated from a YAML file*

This process might seem a convoluted way to add in standard navigation, but in reality, it's much simpler than it sounds! To see what I mean, let's dive into our next exercise and take a look at what is involved in more detail.

ADDING IN NAV LINKS

To see how to add in navigation links, follow these steps:

1. The first step is to navigate to the `header.ejs` file is in your blog's theme, in the `\themes\landscape\layout\_partial` folder. The file type is an Embedded JavaScript template, so it should open without issue in your text editor.

2. We need to add in a little JavaScript to process the menu tags we entered in an earlier file. Crack open a new file in your text editor, and then go ahead and add in this code:

```
<div class="blog-masthead">
  <div class="container">
    <nav class="blog-nav">
      <% for (var i in theme.menu){ %>
        <a class="blog-nav-item" href="<%- url_for(theme.menu[i]) %>">
        <%= i %></a>
      <% } %>
    </nav>
  </div>
</div>
```

3. Save the file and close it – if you revert back to your browser and refresh the page, you should see something akin to that shown in Figure 3-7.

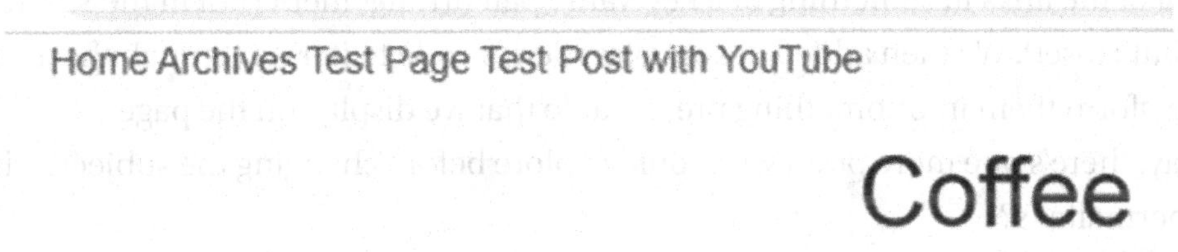

Home Archives Test Page Test Post with YouTube

Coffee

Figure 3-7. Our new navigation links

If we had wanted to keep our menu content separate, then we would need to do the following:

1. Save the same menu entries from before, but this time into a file called `menu.yml`; this needs to be located in the `data` subfolder under the `_source` folder.

2. Add the following code into the layout.ejs file, as a replacement for `<%- partial('_partial/menu') %>` at line 15:

```
<% for (var i in theme.menu){ %>
  <a class="blog-nav-item" href="<%- url_for(theme.menu[i]) %>"><%= i %></a>
<% } %>
```

This will show the content from the `menu.yml` file, instead of the theme's `_config.yml` file.

A relatively simple change, but an important one – now we have the means to navigate around our site correctly! It doesn't matter where we add our links per se – the best way to do it is to get familiar with each of the files (or partials) in the theme folder, so you can match up where you want to add links, with the compiled code in the browser.

There are some key takeaways from this change that we should examine in more detail, so let's take a moment to review the code in more detail.

Understanding the changes

Setting up navigation links is a two-part process in Hexo – the first part is to specify the raw content that is our link list (which we did earlier), and the second will be to transform it into something rendered as part of our theme.

We've already added our menu entries to the theme's `_config.yml` file, where we listed all of the links in something of a key-value pair arrangement (not in the strictest sense, but close!). We then added in some JavaScript code to iterate through these links and transform them into something presentable that we display on the page.

Okay, there's one more point we should explore before changing the subject: what about permalinks?

Using permalinks

"Permalinks?" I hear you ask. "What are they...?"

For some of you, this might not be a new topic, but for the uninitiated, permalinks are what they may sound like: a link that won't change for some considerable time. An excellent example of this is on the Stack Overflow site; permalinks are available for each comment, which makes it easier to reference rather than using the longer standard address.

Hexo is no different: it's very straightforward to set up such a permalink format in your blog. We can change the permalink in either one of two places – in your `_config.yml` file (as a global change) or individually in the front matter for a post (useful if you only want a selection of posts to have links, not all). We can specify a mix of values for our permalink structure – this might be anything from `:year` to `:day` or even `:hour`. The full list is available at `https://hexo.io/docs/permalinks`.

To see how we set permalinks, let's crack on with our next exercise – for this, I will use the global method as a start, but will indicate where we might change content on a per-post basis.

SETTING A PERMALINK

To change the permalink format in use, follow these steps – I assume your Hexo server is not running, so make sure this is the case before you continue:

1. The changes are all in the main `_config.yml` file – so go ahead and crack this open in your text editor and scroll down to this line: permalink: `:year/:month/:day/:title/`.

2. Delete from (and including) :year to the end – replace it with `:category/:title`.

3. Save the file – once done, revert to the Node.js terminal session that you had open for your Hexo server.

4. At the prompt, enter hexo `clean && hexo generate` and then press Enter, to recreate your blog content.

5. Once complete, enter `hexo server -no-optional` to restart your server. You should now see your site; click any blog post title to see your new permalink structure in use.

Although this is a simple change to make, making changes to permalink content is something we do need to consider with some care. The format we use will depend on factors such as date validity (is the content likely to go out of date or be timeless) and the length of the original URL (the shorter the URL, the easier it is to use!). In this example, we've switched to using a straightforward category and title of a post, but you can use whichever format suits your content best.

We can even set up multiple-language support for permalinks – I will show you how in Chapter 8 when we explore the subject of localizing content.

Summary

Wow! That was a lot of information to cover! Building a theme isn't a five-minute job; there is always plenty to consider during development. We've touched on some of the core elements that go to make up a theme; let's take a moment to review what we have learned.

We kicked off by learning how to change themes from the default to something different. We then explored the basic principles behind how we construct a theme, before creating the folder and file structure for our test theme. Next up came a quick look at how we can use variables in themes, before starting to put together the various files that form the basis of our theme.

We then rounded out this part of our journey through creating themes by exploring how to add in navigation – something I'm sure you will agree is vital to any site! We still have loads more to cover, though, before our theme is complete; stay with me as we look at adding widgets, comments, and more in the next chapter.

CHAPTER 4

Developing Themes

Take a look back at the start of Chapter 3. Remember how I said that creating our own theme opens up a world of possibilities and that we can customize it to our needs? Fast-forward to now, we have a theme in place...but it's still missing functionality and doesn't look that great – at least not yet!

While that may indeed be true, it is easy to fix – over these next few pages, we'll continue our journey through creating themes, with a look at adding comments, widgets, and the all-important styling. We'll finish it with a peek at how we might publish our content, so let's start with exploring how we might add an option to comment on posts in our blog.

Adding comments

Everyone has a right to an opinion, and blogs are probably one of the best ways to surface one's thoughts on a subject. Typically, you might store such comments in a database backend, but in the case of Hexo, we have to use alternative means.

To see how we might achieve this, let's run through the steps needed to set up Disqus on our site – this is something we ideally would do once our site is ready to be launched to the world at large.

SETTING UP COMMENTS USING DISQUS

To add in comments using the Disqus system, work through these steps:

1. You need to create an account with Disqus – for this, click the Get Started link on the Disqus website at `https://disqus.com`, and then follow the instructions. Disqus will validate your email address as part of this process.

71

© Alex Libby 2020
A. Libby, *Practical Hexo*, https://doi.org/10.1007/978-1-4842-6089-0_4

Make a note of the name given to you by Disqus – this is your shortname and will be critical to configuring some of the steps in this exercise.

2. Once signed up, click I want to install Disqus on my site.

3. Disqus will ask for the name of your site – enter something suitable here. I will use "Test Blog" as an example. Feel free though to change it for something else if you prefer, but take note of the name you use.

4. Next, select a category – choose Tech (or something else, if more appropriate), and then click Create Site.

5. On the next screen, choose Basic as the Plan Type.

6. Disqus will prompt you to choose which platform your site uses. Scroll down to the button marked I don't see....

7. Go ahead and add in this code, immediately before the closing `</div>` in `post.ejs`:

```
<% if (config.disqus_shortname){ %>
<script>
  var disqus_shortname = '<%= config.disqus_shortname %>';
  <% if (page.permalink){ %>
  var disqus_url = '<%= page.permalink %>';
  <% } %>
  (function(){
    var dsq = document.createElement('script');
    dsq.type = 'text/javascript';
    dsq.async = true;
    dsq.src = '//go.disqus.com/<% if (page.comments){ %>embed.js<% }
    else { %>count.js<% } %>';
    (document.getElementsByTagName('head')[0] || document.
    getElementsByTagName('body')[0]).appendChild(dsq);
  })();
</script>
<% } %>
```

8. Crack open the main _config.yml file, then scroll down to the bottom, and add in the following code – see step 2 for your shortname:

```
disqus:
    enable: true
    shortname: YOUR SHORTNAME
```

9. Save both files and close them, and then browse to your blog site at http://localhost:4000 – if all is well, you should have blog comments appear at the bottom of each post page, similar to those shown on the main Hexo website.

Understanding what happened

Adding comments is a crucial part of any blog website – with modern blog systems such as WordPress, it's a cinch to do (and the core part of it is already done for you anyway).

With Hexo, though, it's not quite as straightforward – there are a few more steps involved! In our case, we started by creating a suitable account on the Disqus website, before inserting a (adapted) slice of boilerplate code into the post.ejs file so that comments can be displayed.

It's worth noting that the code has been adapted to only show if comments are present; otherwise, we have the two core elements – a <div id="disqus_thread"></div> element for locating comments and the script block for rendering the comments on-screen. We've also set our Disqus shortname within the _config.yml file so that it can display the right feedback on our site.

If you would like to develop things further, then it may be worth trying out the hexo-comments plugin at https://github.com/andreisbitnev/hexo-comments; I would also suggest trying the additional steps marked on the Universal Install instructions page at https://test-blog-xtawpxkt38.disqus.com/admin/settings/universalcode/.

Adding widgets

"Widget for this, widget for that..."

Does that sound familiar? I frequently heard something similar when the iPad first came out – the number of times people relied on an app to do X or Y was scary!

That aside, if you happen to frequent blogs as much as I do, then you can't fail to notice several features that appear in the sidebar, such as an About Us, list of recent posts, categories, and the like. Hexo is no different – we can add in a host of different widgets for similar purposes. We can set up widgets similarly to partials. With this in mind, let's take a look at the steps to create these widgets in more detail.

SETTING UP WIDGETS

Although we're dealing with widgets, in reality, there is little difference between them and partials; the process is very similar for adding widgets to our site. To see how, let's work through these steps – make sure you stop your Hexo server first:

1. The first widget we will create is an About Us – for this, crack open your text editor, and add the following code to a new file:

```
<% if(theme.widgets.about){ %>
  <div class="sidebar-module">
    <h4>About</h4>
    <p><%- theme.widgets.about %></p>
  </div>
<% } %>
```

2. Save this as about.ejs in the _widget folder. Second, add the following code to a new file, and save this as categories.ejs in the same folder:

```
<% if (theme.widgets.categories){ %>
  <div class="sidebar-module">
  <h4><%= __('Categories') %></h4>
    <div class="widget">
      <%- list_categories({show_count: theme.show_count}) %>
    </div>
  </div>
<% } %>
```

3. The third widget we will add in is to display the tags associated with each post – this requires a little more code. Add the following to a new file, saving it as tags.ejs in the _widget folder:

```
<% if (theme.widgets.tags && site.tags.length){ %>
  <div class="sidebar-module">
    <h4>Tag Cloud</h4>
    <p>
      <% site.tags.sort('name').each(function(item){ %>
        <a href="<%- config.root %><%- item.path %>" style="font-size:
        <%- Math.min(item.posts.length * 4 + 10, 30) %>px"><%= item.
        name %></a>
      <% }); %>
    </p>
  </div>
<% } %>
```

4. The last widget we will add in is an archive list – add the following code to a new file called archives.ejs, in the _widget folder:

```
<% if(theme.widgets.archives){ %>
  <div class="sidebar-module">
    <h4><%= __('Archives') %></h4>
    <div class="widget">
      <%- list_archives({show_count: theme.show_count, type: theme.
      archive_type}) %>
    </div>
  </div>
<% } %>
```

5. With the widgets now in place, it's time to restart the Hexo server – revert to the Node.js terminal session where it was running at the start of this exercise, and then enter hexo clean && hexo generate to recreate our content files.

6. Once done, enter hexo server -no-optional at the prompt to restart – if all is well, we should see something akin to the screenshot in Figure 4-1.

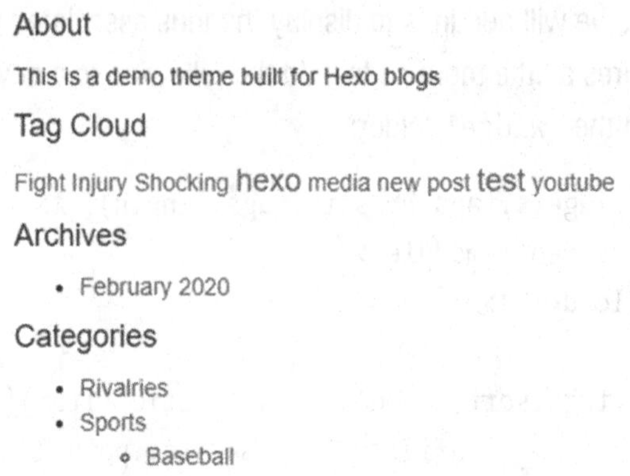

About

This is a demo theme built for Hexo blogs

Tag Cloud

Fight Injury Shocking hexo media new post test youtube

Archives

- February 2020

Categories

- Rivalries
- Sports
  - Baseball

Figure 4-1. *Our (unstyled) widgets in action*

Although this was a straightforward exercise, some of you might notice one small detail missing – how did we tell our site to load the widgets?

It's a good question, and the answer to that lies in the _sidebar.ejs file we created earlier in this chapter. Now's an excellent opportunity to go through the code in more detail. Let's take a moment to do just that, and understand how to hook these widgets into our theme in more detail.

Understanding the code in detail

Although we've built four different widgets, all of them share a similar build process: we first run a check for the presence of the target content; if it's available, we then show the title of our widget and iterate through each item.

In each instance, we use the theme.widgets property to iterate through the type of content we want to display – it might be categories, tags, or potentially archives. If our desired content is present, we then set up a <div> to store each entry; this contains either a hard-coded title or one using the Lodash library to reference it from our _config. yml file. Where things differ slightly is in how we iterate through that content; it might merely be to grab the contents of the property (in the case of theme.widgets.about) or use list_XXXXX to parse the content, where we replace XXXXX with either categories or archives.

The odd one out here is the tag cloud; here we've used .each to iterate through the site.tags property and used it to build a set of different-sized text labels. The key to the latter is in the use of Math.min, which we use to calculate the font size based on the number of posts multiplied by 4. We specify the + 10 to ensure that each answer has a font size of at least 10 px, up to a maximum of 30 px.

To round things off, we go through what should by now be a standard process of regenerating our content pages. We then restart the server to allow for the changes to take effect, although as we've not changed the `_config.yml` file, these last two stages aren't strictly necessary!

Okay, let's move on. There is one more feature we are going to add in for our site, and it is the traditional sitemap. In the past, this was something we might have had to generate from scratch, but thankfully this is not the case; we can use a plugin for this purpose. It's a straightforward install. Let's dive in and take a look at how it works in more detail.

Adding a sitemap

To add a sitemap in Hexo is easy – we have the choice (at the time of writing) of two plugins that we can use for this purpose. Sitemaps are essential for SEO purposes; they give the likes of Google an indication that there is a site out there that it can crawl – whether it is will be up to Google to decide if the quality of the data is sufficient for it to do so!

Leaving the vagaries of SEO management aside, the one I've elected to use for our next exercise is from the main Hexo website, available at `https://github.com/hexojs/hexo-generator-sitemap`. The other one performs a similar role, but includes styling – this isn't necessary for our purposes. Let's take a look at how to get it set up and create that sitemap for our site in more detail.

INSTALLING AND SETTING UP A SITEMAP

To set up the sitemap for our blog, follow these steps:

1. Make sure your blog server is stopped – for this, revert to any Node.js terminal session where the Hexo server is running and press Ctrl+C to stop it.

2. Next, at the prompt, enter this command and press Enter:

```
npm install hexo-generator-sitemap --save
```

3. We need to add in a couple of changes to our theme's `_config.yml` file (not the main one), so crack it open in your text editor and drop the following code in at the end of the file, leaving a blank line after the previous entry:

```
sitemap:
    path: sitemap.xml
    template: ./sitemap_template.xml
    rel: false
```

4. Save the file and close it – back at the terminal session prompt, enter `hexo clean && hexo generate` (to make sure we start with up-to-date content), and then press Enter.

5. Finally, enter `hexo server -no-optional` at the prompt, and then press Enter to restart our server.

6. If you take a look in the public folder of our blog, you will see a `sitemap.xml` file is now present (Figure 4-2).

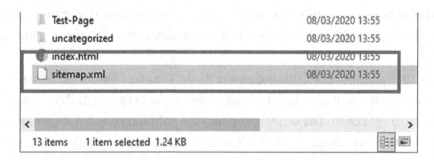

Figure 4-2. *A new sitemap for our site*

Setting up a sitemap was a simple change to make – nevertheless, an important one. Sitemaps are frequently misunderstood (and potentially misused), so anything that we can do that makes it easier to set up means no excuses for us! That aside, there are a couple of configuration details worth examining in more detail, so let's pause for a moment to review the changes made from this exercise.

Breaking apart the changes

To set up a sitemap can be a double-edged sword in some respects – it may make it easier when giving Google an indication of content to be crawled, but at the same time, they must decide that content is worth crawling too!

So, what did we do? Well, much of the hard work was done for us by the plugin. We kicked off by using NPM to install the plugin; this uses a standard install approach, so nothing new. The critical change came when configuring our `_config.xml` file – we used three parameters (`path`, `template,` and `rel`) to set how our plugin stores the file and to link files back to the sitemap.

Okay…enough configuring, methinks. It's time to style our site! You would be forgiven for thinking this has come late in the process, but there's a reason for this; the style rules that we will use cover all of the content, including the widgets that are on the page. Let's dive in and see if we can turn our ugly duckling of a site (one can't but admit that it's not going to win a beauty contest as its stands) into something presentable and usable for future development.

Applying styles

When it comes to styling in Hexo, I suspect you may be thinking this could be complicated; it's a case of dividing styles among different folders or perhaps having to use a preprocessor to write our code and so on…

Well, I hate to disappoint, but it is far easier than you might expect! Before we take a look at the technical details, let me tempt you with a preview of the final article, as shown in Figure 4-3.

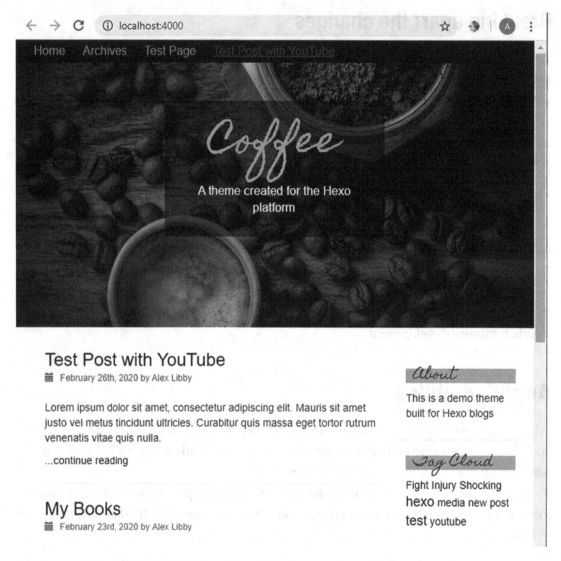

Figure 4-3. *Our completed theme, with styling applied*

Adding in styles is easy in Hexo, in that there are only two things you need to remember: where to put the files and to regenerate the files every so often, to reflect any updates you make to the source files.

With this in mind, let's take a look at the first point around storing our content; Figure 4-4 shows where CSS style sheets and media should be located.

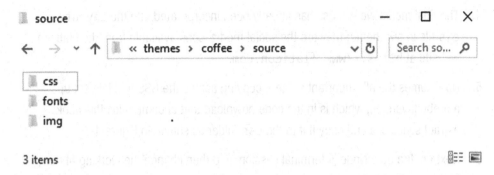

Figure 4-4. *Contents of the theme's source folder*

Inside this folder, we can store each media according to its type – in this case, `fonts`, `css`, and `img` for fonts, styles, and images, respectively. The key to making this work though is in the regeneration process; when we run `hexo clean && hexo generate`, this will delete the contents of the public folder (stored at the root of our blog site) and recreate it from scratch.

With this in mind, let's run through the steps needed to complete the styling for our theme in more detail.

FINALIZING OUR THEME'S STYLING

To update the styling for this theme, follow these steps – make sure you've stopped your Hexo server first, before continuing:

1. The first step is to download a copy of the image we will use for the header in our theme – for this, browse to `https://www.pexels.com/photo/white-ceramic-mug-filled-with-coffee-beside-coffee-beans-678654/`, and click the Download ➤ Large option to download the image.

2. Go ahead and create a folder called `img` (as indicated in Figure 4-4), to store the image inside the source folder of our theme.

3. For our theme, we'll make use of a custom font; I've elected to use Homemade Apple, which is a rustic script-based font. It's available from `https://www.fontsquirrel.com/fonts/homemade-apple`; go ahead and download it from the Webfont Kit link on this page. The download contains a WOFF format font file; this needs to be stored inside a new fonts folder, as indicated in Figure 4-4.

4. The final media we will use has already been incorporated into the `layout.ejs` file in our theme; they are the social media icons available from the FlatIcon website at `https://www.flaticon.com`.

5. Now comes the all-important stage – copying across the CSS file! I've set up a prebuilt version, which is in the code download that accompanies this book; extract styles.css and copy it into the `css` folder as shown in Figure 4-4.

6. Next up, fire up a Node.js terminal session, and then change the working folder to the `myblog` folder.

7. At the prompt, enter `hexo clean && hexo generate` to recreate our files with the updated media.

8. Next, enter `hexo server -no-optional` at the prompt and press Enter; if you browse to `http://localhost:4000`, you should see something akin to the screenshot shown at the start of this exercise.

Congratulations! We now have a working theme – yes, it probably is a little simple, and there are things we can do to develop it, but as they say, we have to start somewhere. Although it appears we've made some radical changes to our blog, in reality, we've just added in an image, a font file, and a prebuilt style sheet – nothing complicated at all!

Testing our theme

Before we can release our code to the wild, there are two critical steps left for us to complete – we need to test it, and (assuming nothing stops us) get it online for others to see!

Hexo does have a formal process for testing, but it isn't what some of you might expect – it's not a case of running unit testing using libraries or frameworks such as Jest or Cypress, but something a little simpler!

The current process relies more on using a published checklist to make sure we maintain a certain level of consistency; we have to spin up a dummy blog, before installing a copy of our theme and working through the list. It's not a complex list, but I would recommend taking a peek at it before you start developing a theme – it contains the core areas that should be present in your theme and will serve as a useful starting point for developing future themes! With this in mind, let's take a look at these steps in more detail as part of our next exercise.

```
TESTING A THEME
```

The standard testing process makes use of the dummy blog site available for installing from `https://github.com/hexojs/hexo-theme-unit-test`. Make sure any current blog site has been stopped, and then work through these steps:

1. First, crack open a Node.js terminal session prompt, and then change the folder to the root of C:

2. Next, enter this command at the prompt, and press Enter: `git clone` `https://github.com/hexojs/hexo-theme-unit-test.git`

   You will see something akin to the screenshot shown in Figure 4-5.

```
Node.js command prompt                                                      —    □    ×

C:\>git clone https://github.com/hexojs/hexo-theme-unit-test.git
Cloning into 'hexo-theme-unit-test'...
remote: Enumerating objects: 167, done.
Receiving objects:  48% (81/167)sed 0 (delta 0), pack-reused 167 eceiving objects:  47% (79/167)
Receiving objects: 100% (167/167), 1.52 MiB | 3.53 MiB/s, done.
Resolving deltas: 100% (87/87), done.

C:\>
```

Figure 4-5. *Cloning the test blog site, ready for testing*

3. Once done, create a new folder called `themes` in the `hexo-theme-unit-test` folder that you've just created (as part of the cloning process).

4. Go ahead and copy the contents of the `coffee` theme folder from our blog to the new `themes` folder.

5. Fire up your text editor, then look for the theme: entry in the **main** `_config.yml` file, and change the word landscape to `coffee`.

6. Next, revert to your Node.js terminal session, and change the working folder to the `hexo-theme-unit-test folder`.

7. At the prompt, enter `npm install` to set up any dependencies.

8. Next, enter `hexo start server -no-optional`, and then browse to the blog at `http://localhost:4000` – you should now see your new theme running on the dummy site.

9. Follow the steps outlined at `https://github.com/hexojs/hexo-theme-unit-test`, to check through your theme. If all is good, then we can publish our theme (we'll work through the steps on how to achieve this shortly).

After most of the exercises we've completed thus far, we've worked through the changes in more detail. This time around, I'm going to break with tradition and not do that; let me explain why.

In this last exercise, we've not made any changes per se; these may well come once you've worked through the aforementioned checklist. The critical thing here, though, is that we're testing our theme on a separate blog; this ensures we can move the theme without breaking it (as a result of not installing any missing dependencies or forgetting to copy across ancillary folders needed for our theme).

Okay, let's move on. We've finally reached the last part of our journey through creating themes, but why keep them to yourself when others may like them and want to use them? Assuming we can release them, and that they are indeed ready to be published, let's have a look at the steps involved in releasing our theme to the wild.

Publishing themes online

The best way to publish a theme is via the library on the main Hexo website at `https://hexo.io/docs/themes`. For this, we need a GitHub account and a means to edit images; the rest we already have installed, or we can use existing tools.

The essential steps are straightforward, although how we will carry them out will depend on whether you use a GUI-based tool or the command line. Let's take a look at what we need to do to get our theme made available online.

As our theme is likely to require further development, we will only cover the steps in theory; we should complete them once the theme is ready for release.

PUBLISHING THEMES ONLINE

If you're at the stage where you're ready to release your work online, then you can use these steps to publish your work:

1. The first step is to fork the Hexo site – for this, browse to `https://github.com/hexojs/site`, then sign in with your account details, and click the Fork button toward the top right of the screen.

2. Next, we need to clone the repository to your computer and install dependencies. For this, fire up a terminal session (the Node.js one is fine); then at the prompt, enter these commands, in turn pressing Enter after each:

```
git clone https://github.com/<username>/site.git
cd site
npm install
```

3. We now need to create a `themes.yml` file, which we store in the `/source/_data/` folder. Crack open a text editor, and add the following to a new file, adjusting each to suit your new theme:

```
- name: landscape
  description: A brand new default theme for Hexo.
  link: <link to your theme's GitHub page>
  preview: <link to a URL showing a preview of the theme>
  tags:
    - official
    - responsive
    - widget
    - two_column
    - one_column
```

4. We have almost finished with making changes – we need to add a screenshot of our theme, which should have the same name, into the `source/themes/screenshots` folder. It must be in PNG format, of a size of 800 px × 500 px.

5. We can now push the changes up to the Hexo site – go ahead and enter the following command in a terminal session, and then press Enter:

```
git push origin master
```

6. All that remains is to create a pull request and describe the change – once merged in, you will be able to see your new theme on display for others to use and download at their convenience.

Success! We've built our theme and styled it, and we can now make it available when we're happy to release it for others online! We've covered a lot of useful content throughout this chapter; it's worth noting though that we've only managed to scratch the surface of what is possible in theme development.

Don't worry, though – there are a host of other areas we can investigate to help develop and improve our theme! Any theme we develop will, of course, be shaped according to our needs – to help give you some inspiration, I've put together some ideas for you in the form of a question: "Where do we go next?"

Where next?

Yes, indeed, where can we go with developing Hexo themes? Well, there are plenty of possibilities; to get you started, here are a few ideas:

- An easy concept to begin with – how about browsing through the themes listed in the Hexo theme library at `https://hexo.io/themes/`? Granted, some may have been around a few years, but I'll bet there will be something there to inspire you!

- It's important not to forget that Hexo, being based on JavaScript and NPM, can also support using appropriate plugins from the NPM library. You may find it more suited to tasks that we should perform outside of Hexo, such as compressing images, but it's something to keep in mind when working with Hexo.

- A significant area to consider is caching – we've focused on developing the essential constituents of our theme in this chapter. I would recommend exploring how caching could help before moving your theme into production use. As a start, I would look at `https://hexo.io/docs/templates#Optimization` – it's easy to implement, although the hard part is where, not how!

- Hexo supports a wide variety of different variables and helpers, such as site and config or adding in favicons; this includes making use of the Lodash library (`https://lodash.com`). We've only touched on the basics in this chapter, but I would recommend having a look at the Lodash library, `https://hexo.io/docs/variables`, and `https://hexo.io/docs/helpers` to see if your theme could benefit from using some of the options listed.

- Throughout this chapter, we've used a few plugins to help, such as helping to set up a sitemap or compiling Sass code (when we initially changed over the theme at the start). Hexo has a good list of plugins available at `https://hexo.io/plugins/` – it's worth taking a look to see if any could help with developing your theme. After all, why reinvent the wheel if someone has already done it for you?

That's a good list of ideas – I am sure there will be something in there to help you develop your themes and to make more of what Hexo can offer in this arena. It goes without saying that what you use will, of course, be dictated by your requirements, but hopefully, there are a few suggestions there that will help you when you come to develop more themes for Hexo in the future.

Summary

Creating a theme is by no means a simple, five-minute affair – there is plenty to think about, and we've only scratched the surface of what is possible! We've covered a fair amount of content in these last two chapters; let's take a moment to review what we have learned.

We took up from where we left off in Chapter 3, with an overview of how we can add in comments, using the Disqus system. This discussion was then followed by working through creating some simple widgets and generating a sitemap with a Hexo plugin, before finishing off with adding styles.

We then rounded out the chapter with a discussion on testing our theme, before having a look through the various steps required to publish our theme online for others to download and use in their blogs.

At this stage, we have the basis for a decent blog, with our custom-built theme. This is great; there may well be a time when we want to take things further. We could use a plugin, but that might be overkill for our needs. What do we do? Well, Hexo has a great API that's perfect for adding custom features – stay with me as we take a look at how it works and answer the question "When is a plugin not a plugin?" in the next chapter.

CHAPTER 5

Working with the API

Up until now, we've started to develop our blog by adding media, content, and the like. Developing our blog in this manner is perfect, but there may come a time when we want to take things further and – to coin a phrase – "spice things up a little."

One way to achieve this is through the use of plugins; Hexo has an excellent plugin capability, but this might not be enough. Instead, we can take things further by making use of its API – this allows us to custom tasks or even develop plugins to help automate processes and make our lives easier.

For this chapter and the next, we'll explore the world of the Hexo API, before taking a look at some of the plugins available and how we can use them, and creating our own that we can publish online for others to use.

But…when is a plugin not a plugin?

Ask any developer this question, and the answer they give might seem a little confused – after all, a plugin is a plugin, surely?

Well, in some respects, yes – and no. From a purely technical perspective, a plugin file might well have the necessary code structure in place and resemble a plugin. However, when using Hexo, there is an important distinction we need to make. Let me explain what I mean by this.

Although Hexo has a well-established API, it's essential to note that we can add this functionality in several ways. We have features like filters and generators (more in a moment), but more importantly, we have options such as helpers, tags, and plugins.

The reason I've highlighted these last three is simple – the one to use will depend on the following: (a) are we targeting source files, and (b) how much code are we adding? Let's explore what this means in reverse.

© Alex Libby 2020
A. Libby, *Practical Hexo*, https://doi.org/10.1007/978-1-4842-6089-0_5

If we need to add in what turns out to be more than just a few lines of code, then I would recommend using a plugin; the other two are designed more for simple snippets of code that are no more than a few lines long. There is no hard-and-fast rule, but I would suggest taking a look at the source code of some of the plugins at `https://hexo.io/plugins/` to get a feel for what is acceptable.

On the other hand, if we just want to insert a small piece of markup, then tags or helper files should be used. Both use a very similar syntax, but the key difference is that we can't use the latter in any markdown file that sits in the source folder.

Okay, let's crack on. With this in mind, it's time we took a look at the features available in the Hexo API and began to explore using them in action.

Exploring what is available in Hexo

If you were to take a look at the documentation on the main Hexo website at `https://hexo.io/api/`, you might be asking yourself where to start – there is a whole host of options available! The truth be told, it can seem a little daunting; the features you choose to use will, of course, depend on what you want to achieve, so let's summarize what is available.

In short, we can split elements of the API into two camps – one to cover the core functionality and the other as extensions.

Core and extension features are just the start, though, as we have more advanced features available for referencing specific instances of Hexo – we will take a look at those later in this chapter.

We can see the list of core API functions available for Hexo in Table 5-1.

Table 5-1. *List of core options*

Feature	Details
Events	Used to fire or respond to events in Hexo – we can respond to events using the `on` method and trigger them using the `emit` method.
Locals	Used for rendering templates, using the `site` variable.
Router	This API function saves all of the routes (or links to pages) that we use on the site.
Box	The Box object acts as a container for processing files in a targeted folder; this might be `hexo.source` for source files (i.e., blog posts, pages, etc.) or `hexo.theme` for theme files.
Rendering	We can use this to render files into static markup, using either the asynchronous `hexo.render.render` method or the synchronous `hexo.render.renderSync` method.
Posts	We can use the `hexo.posts` object to create, render, or publish posts.
Scaffolds	We touched on creating scaffolds earlier in the book; we can use this API call to get the currently set scaffold, change it, or remove it entirely.
Themes	An essential part of operating a blog is to set a theme; we can create different views of the same theme, for a specific use or to allow for desktop or mobile applications. We can then use the `hexo.theme` property to get, set, or remove a view from use within our blog. API documentation: `https://hexo.io/api/themes`

All of the API documentation is available as links from `https://hexo.io/api`.

In contrast, we also have several extensions available for use in Hexo – Table 5-2 lists a summary of the options available.

Table 5-2. *List of available extensions*

Extension	Details
Migrator	We can use this API function to migrate data from different platforms into something suitable for use in Hexo – this is something we will explore more in Chapter 11. API documentation: `https://hexo.io/api/migrator`
Generator	We use generators to compile a list of routes to specific page types, based on processed files; this is perfect for instances such as creating an author index that links to individual author pages, using a predetermined layout. API documentation: `https://hexo.io/api/generator`
Console	The console extension acts as a bridge between Hexo and its users, by making console commands available to Hexo. API documentation: `https://hexo.io/api/console`
Deployer	We can use this API object to deploy a site to a remote server – we will explore deployment more in Chapter 7. API documentation: `https://hexo.io/api/deployer`
Filter	Filters are a technique that originated from WordPress – they are used to modify specific data, such as turning a username into a link to its Twitter profile. API documentation: `https://hexo.io/api/filter`
Helper	Helpers are useful for adding quick snippets of code to non-source pages, such as inserting script links or (as we've seen) adding Google Fonts. API documentation: `https://hexo.io/api/helper`
Processor	Processors are used to process selected files and are part of the Box object for Hexo. We can specify which data to process and the action to take, such as creating, updating, or deleting targeted files. API documentation: `https://hexo.io/api/box`
Tag	Tags are useful for inserting snippets of code into posts – such as markup for the new <audio> tags. API documentation: `https://hexo.io/api/tag`
Renderer	Renderers are for processing certain types of content, where we pass in a file name, the output name, and the action to take on the content. A perfect example is for those of us who like using CSS preprocessors such as Sass or Stylus – we'll work through an example using Sass later in this chapter.

Wow! There is indeed a fair amount of choice available for us! I would recommend taking a look at the documentation on the main Hexo website, though, as each offers several properties or methods that we can use with each feature.

Enough of the theory, though – it's time we got stuck into some code! We're going to dedicate this chapter to explore how some of these features work; I've chosen three as our targets, namely, helpers, tags, and generators. We'll make a start with helpers; these are small and designed to do pretty much as the label says on the tin (to – badly – misquote that famous expression)...

Making use of Hexo helpers

So, what are helpers? Put simply, they are a quick way of adding in snippets of code to your site, where you might include a block of markup multiple times or link to style sheets that are in a specific folder.

Hexo comes with a lengthy list of helpers already included – you can see the full list at `https://hexo.io/docs/helpers`.

Yes, we can add in links to style sheets (or even script files) manually – there's nothing technically wrong with this approach. But if we find ourselves repeating the same operation, why add in the code multiple times when we can add it in once and get Hexo to do the heavy lifting for us?

If we decide to use a helper, there are a few things we should bear in mind:

- We store helpers within the scripts folder inside of a theme folder; when they run as part of generating blog content, Hexo renders the results in the public folder at the root of the blog folder, not in the theme folder.

- We can't use helpers from our markdown source files.

- Helpers can make use of any one of a host of variables already built into Hexo, such as site, page, or config; a list of these is available at `https://hexo.io/docs/variables`.

A critical point we need to allow for is deciding when a helper is not a helper and should be a plugin. There is no hard-and-fast rule, but a good indicator is to consider complexity. If all you want to do is insert a link, then a helper is perfect; something more complex such as adding in Font Awesome (which is in itself adding links) should be a plugin!

With this in mind, let's take a look at how helpers work in more detail, with a simple exercise to add in fonts from the online Google Fonts repository.

Creating a custom helper

Hands up how many times you've added something akin to the following code snippet in any of your projects?

```
<link href="https://fonts.googleapis.com/css2?family=Open+Sans&display=sw
ap" rel="stylesheet">
```

I'll bet there will be a few of you who have at some point in the past – you will, of course, recognize this as (in)famous Google Fonts! Typically, we might have had to write this entire line in as part of adding it to our markup; that is an old-school ball-ache of a pain to do! The font name may change, but the basic link principle doesn't; why not get Hexo to do it for you?

Absolutely! With a bit of work, we can quickly turn this into a helper, so that all we need to provide is the name of our Google-hosted font. To see what I mean, we're going to do that in our next exercise; I've chosen to use the Open Sans font, but this will work with any font hosted by Google.

ADDING GOOGLE FONTS WITH A HELPER

To see how using a helper can be a real time-saver for using Google Fonts, stop your Hexo server, and then follow these steps:

1. First, crack open a new file in your text editor, and add in this code, saving it as googlefonts.js in the /theme/coffee/scripts folder:

```
hexo.extend.helper.register('gf', function(fontname){
    return '<link href="https://fonts.googleapis.com/css2?family=' +
    fontname + '&display=swap" rel="stylesheet">';
});
```

2. Next, open the `layout.ejs` file – go ahead and remove `<%- js('/js/abc.js') %>` and then add this below the second `<link>` statement:

    ```
    <%- gf('Open Sans') %>
    ```

3. Save and close any files you have open, and then run this command from a Node.js terminal session, to regenerate the blog files:

    ```
    hexo clean && hexo generate && hexo server
    ```

4. When prompted, go ahead and browse to `http://localhost:4000`. We should see our blog remains unchanged, but if we open the browser's developer console area, we will see the addition of our chosen Google font, as indicated in Figure 5-1.

```
<link rel="stylesheet" href="https://maxcdn.bootstrap
4.5.0/css/font-awesome.min.css">
<link href="https://fonts.googleapis.com/css2?
family=Open+Sans&display=swap" rel="stylesheet"> == $
<link rel="stylesheet" href="/css/styles.css">
<meta name="generator" content="Hexo 4.2.0">
```

Figure 5-1. *The addition of a Google font using a helper*

It's at this point that we can then make use of it in our CSS styling file, should we wish – it doesn't matter which font we call in from Google, as we can add them using the same technique.

Making use of helper files is a great time-saver; have you noticed how, in the last exercise, we added in different functions, but that the principle of storing the files is the same? It is a useful technique to master, so let's take a moment to go through what we achieved in the last exercise in more detail.

Breaking apart the code

Assembling a helper can be a double-edged sword in some respects – they are designed to be quick and easy to add snippets of code, but only really useful if we can reuse them multiple times in our blog (or across various blogs). Leaving this consideration aside for a moment, creating a helper is a simple task, but one which raises a critical point that we should consider, so let's dive in and take a look at the code in more detail.

We kicked off by creating our helper as a standard JavaScript file within the scripts folder of our theme. This follows a standard format of hexo.extend.helper.register, where we pass in the name of the helper before executing the function that contains our helper. In this instance, we returned a link that points to the appropriate font on Google Fonts' website, in the same way we would import this font manually into any HTML markup.

We then referenced that helper from within the layout.ejs file, by calling gf and passing into it the name of our chosen font. As the final step, we ran the (by now) familiar Hexo clean, generate, and server commands, to regenerate our content and restart the server so the updated content can be displayed on-screen.

The key point to remember though is that although we store the helper within the theme/scripts folder, the results of it are only shown in the *public* folder at the time of generating our static content. This might sound a little confusing, but the best way to treat it is that Hexo collects together everything from different sources (or folders), before processing each and rendering the output to the public folder.

Okay, let's crack on. We've created a custom helper, which is great, but: one of the drawbacks of using them is that they don't work inside source files. This potentially means we're missing out on a large chunk of material which could be customized!

Thankfully, this isn't an issue though, as we can add in custom functionality – instead of using helpers, we have to use tags. These allow us to add in similar features to posts; let's dive in and explore these in more detail.

Creating tag snippets

When working with posts, we can add in all manner of different options – if you're familiar with blogging, then one option might be to style a block of text as a code excerpt, or for more scholarly endeavors where we need to quote an author, we might put in a block quote.

In all instances, tags follow a specific format – we have to reference an instance of Hexo, by extending and registering a specific tag, thus:

```
hexo.extend.tag.register(name, function(args, content){
  // ...
}, options);
```

Once created (and stored in the scripts folder of our theme), we can reference the tag using this format:

```
{% <name of tag> <any properties that need to be passed> %}
```

Let's put this to good use, by creating a tag for adding in a tag to add in markup for HTML5 audio files automatically, as part of our next demo. For this, you will need to have a file of suitable format to hand – a perfect example is something from iTunes if you use this (which is M4A format), or I am sure you can find something online that will work.

Assuming you have something available, let's crack on with the demo.

CREATING TAG SNIPPETS

Make sure your Hexo server is stopped, and then run through these steps. I will assume you're using the Coffee theme we created earlier; if you're using a different name, then change any instance of coffee as appropriate:

1. First, crack open your text editor, and then add the following code to a new file, saving it as `audiofile.js` in the `/themes/coffee/scripts` folder:

    ```
    hexo.extend.tag.register('audio', function(args){
      var id = args[0];
      return '<audio src="' + id + '" controls></audio>';
    });
    ```

2. Next, choose a post we created earlier – it's doesn't matter which one, as long as it is a post (not a page). I will use one I created earlier called "My Books."

3. Go ahead and open the post's markdown file in your editor (you will find it in the source folder, named after the post title) – pick a paragraph, and then insert this code, replacing `Overture.m4a` with the name and extension of your music file:

    ```
    {% audio './media/Overture.m4a' %}
    ```

4. Make sure you insert a free line before and after, as indicated in Figure 5-2.

```
Vestibulum euismod justo eget velit venenatis,
eu nisl eu lectus egestas luctus at a ex. Nunc

{% audio './media/Overture.m4a' %}

Donec tincidunt vel ligula nec tincidunt. In mi
```

Figure 5-2. *Inserting our audio tag*

5.   Save the file, then switch back to a Node terminal session, and enter this
     command at the prompt and press Enter:

     `hexo clean && hexo generate && hexo server -no-optional`

6.   Assuming all is OK, browse to `http://localhost:4000`, and navigate
     to your chosen post. You should see an audio player appear, as indicated in
     Figure 5-3.

Vestibulum euismod justo eget velit venenatis, et aliquet quam
luctus at a ex. Nunc vitae ligula enim.

Donec tincidunt vel ligula nec tincidunt. In mi lectus, maximus n
Vestibulum non eros id nunc feugiat mattis.

Figure 5-3. *Our newly inserted audio file*

In this example, we've used the same format as from the Google Fonts exercise; it's
a quick way of adding in content, particularly if it is going to be repeated in multiple
instances throughout our blog. There are a couple of important points to note though,
especially around where we store the script and how it is referenced; let's take the
opportunity to break apart our code to see how it works in detail.

Understanding the code in detail

Hexo is blessed with some useful functionality, an example of which are tags; this works in an almost identical manner to the helpers we created in an earlier exercise! This said, there are a couple of key differences, so let's pause for a moment to review our code in more detail.

We started by creating our tag in the same way as we did for the helper – it is stored in the same location, but uses the `hexo.extend.tag.register` method instead. We then edited one of our posts to insert the call to the tag using {%...%}; inside it we passed in the name of our tag, followed by the name of our audio file.

The key difference here though is that tags are designed to work on blog posts, whereas helpers can't be used in source files. Outside of this, we still have to run the familiar Hexo `clean`, `generate`, and `server` commands to allow our content to be updated and rendered correctly on-screen.

Taking into account tag plugins

At some point, you may come across tag plugins, which are available from `https://hexo.io/docs/tag-plugins`.

They look as though they offer the same functionality, but this is not the case! Okay, I know this sounds a little contradictory, but this is because the code used is structured in a different way from standard helpers or tags. You can see some examples of how they are structured at `https://github.com/hexojs/hexo/tree/master/lib/plugins/tag`; if you're feeling adventurous, why not see if you can convert any to be a simple tag?

Okay, let's move on. There is one more area we should explore, which is the use of generators. These are a little more involved, but can be used to generate content based on links throughout our blog. A great example is building an archive page based on all of the posts in our blog. Let's take a moment to explore this crucial feature in more detail, to see what it means in practice.

Adding content through generators

So far, we've touched on using helpers and tags. The third type of functionality we're going to explore are Hexo generators. "Generators – what are they, and what role do they play?" I hear you ask. They are both good questions; the main site's documentation does seem a little sparse on this subject!

They do largely as the name sounds; they can be used to generate content, although there are specific use cases. Before we explore how they might be used, let's first take a look at some example code for a generator:

```
hexo.extend.generator.register(function(locals) {
  return {
    path: "CNAME",
    data: this.config.url.replace(/^(http|https):\/\//, "")
  };
});
```

As you can see, they follow a very similar format to both tags and helpers – it's easy to think that they could even be treated as plugins, but this is not the case! Plugins use a different architecture in Hexo, although at a basic level, they do add functionality in a similar fashion.

In this instance, we use the `hexo.extend.generator` object – we pass into it the `locals` argument, which is a reference to site variables throughout the blog. It's important to note that we should only use this argument; it avoids any risk associated with accessing the `db.json` file directly (which is considered bad practice for Hexo).

Now that we've seen how a generator might look, let's put it to use – I would say we're going to create something, but this time we're going to use a third-party generator. This one is `hexo-generator-cname`, which is available from `https://github.com/leecrossley/hexo-generator-cname/` and was created by Lee Crosley. It is a very simple one that creates a CNAME file, which is needed for deployment of Hexo sites into production.

ADDING CONTENT THROUGH GENERATORS

Make sure your Hexo server is stopped, and then run through these steps:

1. Crack open a Node.js terminal session, and then change the working folder to `myblog`.

2. At the prompt, enter this command and press Enter:

   ```
   npm install hexo-generator-cname --save-dev
   ```

3. Once installed, enter hexo `clean && hexo generate && hexo server`, and then press Enter, to regenerate files and restart the blog.

4. Go ahead and browse to http://localhost:4000 – we won't see any change, but a check in your file explorer will show a CNAME file listed in the /public folder (Figure 5-4).

Test-Page	29/03/2020 19:21	
uncategorized	29/03/2020 19:21	
CNAME	29/03/2020 19:21	
index.html	29/03/2020 19:21	
sitemap.xml	29/03/2020 19:21	

Figure 5-4. *Checking for the presence of a CNAME file*

This was indeed a quick exercise, but nevertheless an important one. CNAME files play an important role when it comes to deploying content into production. The code required for this generator to operate is very straightforward – let's take a look at it in more detail.

Breaking apart the code

This last exercise was so quick it almost hardly warrants an explanation as to what happens! This said, we produced a CNAME file which is needed for the deployment of our site into production (which we will do later in this book).

The code used follows a standard template for all generators, inasmuch as we make use of the hexo.extend.generator object and pass in the locals argument as a placeholder for values consumed inside the generator. All that was returned in this case was the file name CNAME (as the path value) and the URL of our website as the data parameter. It might seem a really easy generator to use, but using it means we are already one step ahead when it comes to deployment!

Okay, we've created some tags and helpers and seen a generator in use. These are all good, but are somewhat limited in the wider scheme of things. We shouldn't forget, though, that one of the dependencies for Hexo is Node.js, so this opens up some real possibilities if we want to push things even further! This means (in theory at least) we can tie in with task runners such as Gulp or add in other Node.js packages such as image optimizer. Great! Or is it...?

Taking things further

When writing this chapter, the title of this section was initially meant to be "Taking things further with Node.js," but I stripped it back to a more generic title for a good reason, as it seems all might not be as good as it should be when using some advanced features of Hexo. Let me explain what I mean by this comment.

Up until now, the examples we've created are great for adding smaller customizations to our content, but they can't be used to change the overall structure of our blog.

For this, we need to use more advanced features from the Hexo API. At the same time, we can also tap in the plugin ecosystem available for Node.js – we've touched on at least one example of using an image optimizer. This is ideal, as it means we can really start to customize how our Hexo blog works – one such target is streamlining the cleaning and generation process, which can be a real pain if you have to enter it more than a few times!

Digging deeper into the API

However, all is not as rosy as it would seem, at least with some of the more advanced options available in the Hexo API. Before I reveal all, let us first take a look at how we would normally work with the API.

The first task is to create an instance of Hexo that by default references our blog (or in the case of multiple blogs being hosted in the same location, the currently active instance). In each instance, we can use standard boilerplate code, similar to this example:

```
var Hexo = require('hexo');
var hexo = new Hexo(process.cwd(), {});

hexo.init().then(function(){
  // ...
});
```

Once this is in place, we can call on the services of a handful of methods. The first is to load() – or watch() – files, followed by executing operations such as hexo. call('list'), before calling hexo.exit() to complete all console commands and tidy up after itself. We could then end up with something akin to this, as an example:

```
var Hexo = require('hexo');
var hexo = new Hexo(process.cwd(), {});

hexo.init().then(function(){
  hexo.call('generate').then(function(){
    return hexo.exit();
  }).catch(function(err){
    return hexo.exit(err);
  });
});
```

With our core API commands in place, we can then further tweak the settings, using any one of a number of options, detailed in Table 5-3.

Table 5-3. *List of configuration options*

Option	Enables...	Default setting
debug	Enables debug mode – debug messages are displayed in the terminal and written to debug.log in the root folder of the blog.	False
safe	Safe mode – no plugins are loaded.	False
silent	Silent mode – no messages are displayed in the terminal.	False
config	Specify the path of the configuration file.	_config.yml
draft / drafts	Sets drafts to be added to the posts list – useful if you use a setting such as hexo.locals.get('posts')	render_drafts of _config.yml

At face value, this seems like a comprehensive setup, right? Unfortunately, not is all as it would seem, at least for Windows users; issues have been reported around using some of these methods, so with that in mind, let's explore these in more detail to get an understanding of how these might affect us in more detail.

The pitfalls of using these API methods

When researching for this book, I tried out several commands – one of which, in particular, caused issues.

The command in question was the watch() command: this is supposed to act to load files, before executing a process to watch for any changes to content. My example file looked like this:

```
var Hexo = require('hexo');
var p = require('path');
var blogsPath = process.cwd();

var hexo = new Hexo(process.cwd());

hexo.init().then(function(){
  hexo.load().then(function() {
    console.log("File changed");
  });
});
```

Saving this to the scripts folder of any theme and executing hexo server did activate it, but with unexpected results! It sent Node and Hexo into a continuous loop, so it was impossible to see if any Hexo registered any changes, and CPU usage shot up by around 40–50%. This quirk is a real problem, so how can we get around this?

Putting a task runner to use

It turns out the best (and most reliable) way was to use a task runner – we can use this to run similar operations, although it's not without its issues. While researching for this book, I came across several problems with using my typical go-to, which is Gulp. This was throwing deprecation warnings and not firing steps in the right order, even we can run though the steps individually! Go figure, as they say...

Instead, I turned to using Grunt – this works very well and produces the results we would expect to see. It does have one sting in the tail, though, but we will come to that in a moment.

For now, let's dive into some code to see how we can set up Grunt to streamline the process needed to regenerate content and restart Hexo. As part of this, we'll make use of the grunt-shell plugin by Sindre Sorhus, available from https://github.com/sindresorhus/grunt-shell – it makes running shell commands much easier!

RESTARTING HEXO

To implement a task runner for restarting Hexo, work through these steps:

1. First, crack open a Node.js terminal session, then enter this command, and press Enter:

```
npm install grunt-cli -g
```

2. Once done, change the current working folder to myblog, and enter this command:

```
npm install grunt --save-dev
```

3. Next, fire up your text editor and add this to a new file, saving it as gruntfile.js in the root of myblog:

```
module.exports = function(grunt) {

  // Project configuration.
  grunt.initConfig({
    shell: {
      clean: {
        command: 'hexo clean'
      },
      generate: {
        command: 'hexo generate'
      },
      startserver: {
        command: 'hexo server -no-optional'
      }
    }
  });

  // Load the plugin that provides the "shell" task.
  grunt.loadNpmTasks('grunt-shell');

  // Default task(s).
  grunt.registerTask('default', ['shell']);
};
```

4. Save this file and close or minimize your editor.

5. Revert to the Node session from earlier, and then run `grunt` at the prompt – if all is well, you should see something akin to Figure 5-5.

```
Done.
Completed in 4.553s at Sun Mar 29 2020 10:50:51 GMT+0100 (British Summer Time) - Waiting...
>> File "source\_posts\hello-world.md" changed.
Running "shell:clean" (shell) task
INFO  Deleted database.
INFO  Deleted public folder.

Running "shell:generate" (shell) task
INFO  Start processing
INFO  Files loaded in 147 ms
INFO  Generated: index.html
INFO  Generated: archives/index.html
INFO  Generated: fancybox/blank.gif
```

Figure 5-5. *Grunt running through steps in gruntfile as a result of a file change*

The use of a task runner here makes it much easier to update files – yes, we can use a plugin such as browsersync, but a task runner allows us to also tap into other Node.js packages, such as minifying images.

We'll look at using browsersync in Chapter 7, as part of optimizing our workflow.

I did allude to something of a sting in this tail though – unfortunately, Gulp isn't entirely an angel either! Thankfully, this isn't too painful a sting, so before we review the code in more detail, let's cover off what this "sting" means for us in practice.

Watching for changes

If we decide to use a task runner or adapt an existing task runner process, then there is something we need to look out for – we can't call the hexo server process we would otherwise have done, as it causes a "port already in use" error.

To get around this, we have to adapt our Grunt file – it means removing the code highlighted in this block:

```
module.exports = function(grunt) {

  // Project configuration.
  grunt.initConfig({
    watch: {
      scripts: {
        files: ['**/*.md'],
        tasks: ['shell'],
        options: {
          interrupt: true,
        },
      },
    },
    shell: {
      clean: {
        command: 'hexo clean'
      },
      generate: {
        command: 'hexo generate'
      },
      startserver: {
        command: 'hexo server -no-optional'
      },
    },
  });

  // Load the plugin that provides the "shell" task.
  grunt.loadNpmTasks('grunt-contrib-watch');
  grunt.loadNpmTasks('grunt-shell');

  // Default task(s).
  grunt.registerTask('default', ['shell']);
};
```

...and that we must run this command separately. It's not ideal, but at least it works; it means we can still automate part of the overall build process, but not all. It's a pain, but a small price to pay for removing some of the grunt work required when working with Hexo!

Compiling Sass code with Hexo

Okay, let's change tack for a moment and create something a little more interesting.

One of the things I love about Hexo is this dependency on Node.js – some might considered it a drag, but we shouldn't. We can hook in all manner of packages to our Hexo blog!

To prove this, and for our next exercise, we're going to explore how to use Hexo renderers. These tools do what they say on the tin; we can use them to process content and render the output. A typical renderer command looks like this:

```
hexo.extend.renderer.register(name, output, function(data, options){
  // ...
}, sync);
```

At a minimum, we need to pass in the source file name (name), a name for the processed output, and the commands we want to run to process our data.

The best way to show how this works is by using it – for our next exercise, we're going to create something to transpile preprocessed styles written in Sass (https://www.sass-lang.com) into standard CSS. We've based our code on one written by Kyle Smith (https://github.com/knksmith57/hexo-renderer-sass). We'll update it though for Dart Sass, which is now the de facto processor for Sass code.

COMPILING SASS CODE

First, make sure you've stopped your Hexo server, and then follow these steps to set it up:

1. First, we need to create a new folder called hexo-renderer-dart-sass – this needs to be inside the node_modules folder at the root of our blog.

2. Next, fire up a Node.js terminal session and change the working folder to the myblog folder.

3. At the prompt, enter this command and press Enter – this will set up a package.json file, ready for us to install our dependencies:

```
npm init -y
```

4. At the prompt, go ahead and enter this command and then press Enter – this will install the Sass NPM package:

```
npm install sass --save-dev
```

5. We need to add in a couple of files – first, add the following code to a new file, and then save it as index.js at the root of the hexo-renderer-dart-sass folder:

```
/* global hexo */
'use strict'

var sassRenderer = require('./lib/renderer')

// associate the Sass renderer with .scss extensions
hexo.extend.renderer.register('scss', 'css', sassRenderer('scss'))
```

6. Next, create a new folder called lib inside the hexo-renderer-dart-sass folder; this is where we will store the code that performs the conversion.

7. Here comes the critical part – go ahead and add the following code to a new file, saving it as renderer.js inside the lib folder we just created:

```
'use strict'
var sass = require('sass')
var extend = require('util')._extend

module.exports = (ext) => function (data) {
  var userConfig = extend(
    this.theme.config.sass || {},
    this.config.sass || {}
  )

  var config = extend({
    data: data.text,
    file: data.path,
    outputStyle: 'nested',
    sourceComments: false
  }, userConfig)
```

```
try {
  var result = sass.renderSync(config);
  return result.css.toString();
} catch (error) {
  console.error(error.toString());
  throw error;
}
}
```

8. There are a couple of changes left to do – the next one is inside the main _
config.yml file, at the root of our blog folder. Open this in your text editor, and
add the code at the bottom of the file (Figure 5-6).

```
113
114    #sass:
115      includePaths:
116        - "./public/css"
```

Figure 5-6. *Editing the _config.yml file to allow Sass compilation*

9. Finally, add the following code to a new file, saving it as test.scss in the /
themes/coffee/ source/css folder:

```
$font-stack: 'homemade_appleregular', sans-serif;
$primary-color: #eab082;

body { font: 100% $font-stack; color: $primary-color; }
```

10. At this point, we're ready to try out compiling our Sass example. Revert to the
Node.js terminal session we hsad open just now; then at the prompt, enter
hexo clean && hexo generate && hexo server to regenerate our blog
files and restart the server.

Although we've run these commands separately until now, Hexo allows us to chain
them together, as shown in this example.

---

11. Go ahead and browse to http://localhost:4000 – if all is well, our blog
will not look any different, but you will see a new test.css file appear in /
public/css (Figure 5-7).

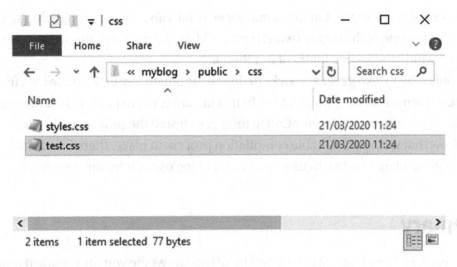

Figure 5-7. Our newly compiled Sass file

Making use of the Hexo API in this way helps open up a host of different avenues for us; we can add in any number of NPM packages, such as compressing images, adding vendor prefixes, or minifying JavaScript files.

Although adding in Sass using this method is straightforward, I suspect there will be at least one question on your lips: how come we're adding the Sass file in the theme, but it appears in the...*public folder*?

Understanding how our code works

Setting up a process such as compiling Sass code is easy enough to do, but is something that does require a little forethought. This demo has highlighted how straightforward it is to create a suitable process; let's take a moment to review the code in more detail.

We started by setting up a suitable folder for our plugin – this included creating a package.json file and installing the latest version of Dart Sass using NPM. We then moved onto creating our renderer as hexo-renderer-dart-sass, before adding in a functions file which would use the Sass NPM package to process our code.

Next up, we had to add in an includePaths folder, to make sure our plugin stored the compiled CSS file in the right location – in this case /public/css, at the root of our blog folder. We then tested our compilation by adding in a test Sass file, before running the now-familiar clean, generate, and server commands to refresh our content and restart the blog.

The locations we've used in this demo for style files are worth noting. Although our content sits outside of the theme (which we would expect anyway), the styles don't; they are stored within the source folder of our theme.

It's only when Hexo `generate` kicks in does it automatically pick up the Sass file and drop the contents into our public folder. In this instance, we've not touched the original `styles.css` file we created for our Coffee theme, so tested the process with a different name. Now that we have a suitable compilation process in place, there is nothing stopping those of us who like to use Sass from making use of it in our Hexo blog!

Summary

When creating a blog, I am sure there will be occasions where you find yourself repeating the same code or wishing there was a shortcut to adding in the same block multiple times – time is precious, and any shortcut has to be a good thing, right? Well, maybe not always, but shortcuts aside, Hexo has no shortage of "shortcuts" we can use. Let's take a moment to review what we've learned in this chapter.

We started by first discussing why adding plugins to our blog may not always be necessary and that sometimes we can achieve the same result with a simple helper or tag. We then moved onto exploring what helpers can offer us, before creating our first helper to import fonts from Google into our blog pages.

Next up, we moved onto creating tag snippets that we can apply to source pages; at the same time, we briefly covered the key point that tag plugins may appear to be similar, but do not act in the same way as standard tags.

We then moved onto creating content through the use of a generator – this time around, we installed a prebuilt generator. We covered how it works, as well as understanding how we will make use of it later in the book.

We then rounded out the chapter with a discourse on using task runners – we explored some of the compatibility issues, before exploring how we can make something work using Grunt as our task runner.

Phew! Another chapter bites the dust, to (mis)quote a famous rock song! Over the course of the last few chapters, we've used a number of Hexo plugins, or at least some that we could consider as pseudo-plugins. It's time we learned how to write them – are you ready to "plug in" and find out how in the next chapter?

CHAPTER 6

Building Plugins

Remember how at the end of the last chapter we created something that uses the Hexo renderer method to compile Sass styling code...?

Take a closer look at the code again – in particular, at the use of the statement npm init -y, plus the use of the line starting with module.exports = (ext) => near the start of the code. What if I said you've created a *plugin*, even though we had intended to create a renderer?

I'll bet you're a little confused by that, and with good reason: Hexo's architecture is such that we can write the core part of a renderer as a script (similar to how we wrote the Google Fonts helper in the previous chapter). It can also be a plugin too – it all depends on how we structure the code. Let's take a moment to revisit a question we asked in Chapter 5 – "When is a plugin not a plugin?" this time from the viewpoint of being a plugin.

When is a plugin not a plugin: Revisited

Back in the previous chapter, we talked briefly about the differences between a plugin, helpers, and tags. We also mentioned that frequently the complexity of the code would determine if we should write it as a plugin or we could get away with it as a helper or tag.

To confuse things further, Hexo also has two types of plugins: tag plugins (you can see details at https://hexo.io/docs/tag-plugins) and standard plugins (a directory of them is available at https://hexo.io/plugins/). The former were ported from Octopress and look and behave more akin to helpers. The latter type are plugins created by others for anyone to download and install as requirements dictate for their projects.

In reality, though, there is a lot of crossover between each type. We can turn helpers and tags into plugins; the latter are helpers or tags with additional configuration options! This crossover makes it confusing to know which route to take when adding in custom

© Alex Libby 2020
A. Libby, *Practical Hexo*, https://doi.org/10.1007/978-1-4842-6089-0_6

functionality – to help remove some of the confusion, we should ask ourselves these questions:

- Do you need to specify choices that could be optional, but equally affect the outcome?

- What type of content will our plugin be targeting? Is it post or page content, or will it operate on content such as CSS styling?

- Is the plugin designed to serve a specific need, or could it be useful to others?

So, taking the hexo-renderer-dart-sass plugin we created from the end of the previous chapter, there are a couple of things that help determine its suitability as a plugin and not as a helper or tag:

- We have several choices that need to be specified, which could affect the outcome; doing this as a plugin is the only feasible option, as it relies on us starting our Hexo server to kick in the transpilation process for our Sass code.

- Although it is possible to use third-party plugins, these would only work if they are used to manipulate content within our posts – such as importing content from an external file. We're not doing that with the hexo-renderer-dart-sass plugin; this affects content that sits outside of posts.

- If it were possible to run the core parts of the hexo-renderer-dart-sass plugin as a helper, then we would have to hard-code the options; not the end of the world, but limiting choices in this way won't appeal to everyone!

Now that we've covered some of the differences from the perspective of a plugin, let's move on – it's a perfect opportunity to take a look at how we should create plugins in Hexo and what we need to have in place to make our plugins work. The great thing about Hexo is that the entry barriers are shallow – it makes it very easy to create a plugin!

Understanding the architecture of a plugin

Yes, indeed, there are only three essential requirements we need to allow for when creating a plugin. Let's take a look at what these requirements are:

- A Hexo plugin must sit in the node_modules folder.

- Inside our plugin folder, we need to have package.json and index.js files.

- All Hexo plugins have to start with hexo-; otherwise, Hexo will ignore them.

The first requirement is almost a given: for any Node.js-based applications, all plugins sit inside the node_modules folder. The second is a default requirement of using NPM, so there is nothing different there; it means that the last one is the only one that is specific to Hexo.

The second requirement though has a couple of points we should consider when it comes to creating and using the package.json file. We do need to specify as a minimum the name, version number, and main entries in the file, although other entries may also appear, depending on what other plugins we use in our plugin:

```
{
  "name": "hexo-renderer-dart-sass",
  "version": "0.0.1",
  "main": "index"
}
```

If we get into the habit of using npm init -y (as we will revisit later in this chapter), then these three are added automatically for us. We do, though, need to make sure we add a reference to the package.json file at the root of our blog folder, so that Hexo knows to include our plugin and load it accordingly.

Okay, let's crack on. We're almost at the point where we can get stuck into code, but before we do so, there is one more topic I want to cover off: the use of existing Hexo tools to accelerate plugin development. We touched on using third-party tools at the end of the last chapter, but Hexo has a few that can equally help – let's take a look at these in more detail.

Using existing tools to accelerate development

When developing a Hexo plugin, we can code the functionality from the ground up or use a third-party plugin to help save time and resource effort while developing code. To help with crafting our plugin, there are four official tools provided (as plugins) by Hexo that we can use:

- hexo-fs – Available from `https://github.com/hexojs/hexo-fs`, this is the file system module for Hexo and is perfect for reading in content from separate files into Hexo.

- hexo-i18n – In this modern age of the Internet, content in different languages is essential. To help with this, Hexo has a localization (i18n) for providing label content in different languages that we can download from `https://github.com/hexojs/hexo-i18n`.

- hexo-pagination – If your plugin relies on paginating content, then this one will help make development easier. It's available from `https://github.com/hexojs/hexo-pagination` and is perfect for generating pagination data.

- hexo-util – If you need to perform tasks such as decoding URLs, stripping HTML markup, or performing pattern matching, then this Swiss Army knife of a plugin is for you. It's available from `https://github.com/hexojs/hexo-util` and is a general-purpose utility plugin for Hexo.

Making use of a third-party plugin can be a double-edged sword – while it can help save time with development, we introduce a dependency on someone else's code. This dependency puts us at the mercy of that author – okay, I know this sounds a little drastic, but it is something we still need to consider! If they stop development, change direction, or implement a feature that introduces a vulnerability, then these can all affect our development.

Writing our first plugin

Okay, we've finally reached the point I know you've all been waiting for: it's time to get stuck into code!

I know it might seem like we've covered a lot of theory, but it's essential to get a good background – jumping straight into coding could mean taking the wrong route to developing your solution and result in you having to redo your work! That aside, it is indeed time to get stuck into coding, so let's make a start with creating our first plugin.

CREATING OUR FIRST PLUGIN

This plugin is based on a version of the hexo-wordcount plugin, available from `https://github.com/willin/hexo-wordcount`; I've simplified it to focus on just displaying the time it takes to read the post and limited it to work on English only.

To set it up, make sure you stop your Hexo server, and then follow these steps:

1. We start by creating our plugin folder – for this, create a new folder called hexo-helper-minread in your node_modules folder within the myblog folder.

2. Next, fire up a Node.js terminal session, then change the working folder to myblog, and enter this command and then press Enter:

   ```
   npm init -y
   ```

3. Once done, switch to your text editor, and then create a new file. We now need to add in our plugin code, which we will do in sections, starting with some variable declarations:

   ```
   var util = require('hexo-util');
   var stripMarkup = util.stripHTML;
   ```

4. This next block creates a function to strip out special characters and odd words
    that may skew the results:

```
var counter = function (content) {
  content = stripMarkup(content);
  const en = (content.match(/[a-zA-Z0-9_\u0392-\u03c9\u0400-\u04FF]
  \w+/g) || []).length; return [en];
};
```

5. We now need to work out how long it will take to read the post – that value is
    handled by this next block:

```
hexo.extend.helper.register('minread', function (content, en = 160) {
  var len = counter(content);
  var readingTime = len[0] / en;
  return readingTime < 1 ? '1' : parseInt(readingTime, 10);
});
```

6. Save the file as index.js.

7. Next, crack open the package.json at the root of your blog folder, and scroll
    to the bottom of the dependencies section. Add in this line before the closing
    bracket:

```
"hexo-helper-minread": "^1.0.0"

},
"devDependencies": {
```

8. Save the package.json file, and close it. Switch to the _config.yml file stored
    in the themes\coffee folder, and add this code into the bottom of that file:

```
plugins:
  hexo-helper-minread
```

9. We're almost done – the last stage before regenerating our content is to call
    our plugin from within the `post.ejs` file. Crack it open in your text editor (it's
    in the `themes/coffee/layout` folder), and modify the code as highlighted:

```
<% if(page.author) { %>
  by <%- page.author %>
  - <span class="post-count"><%- minread(page.content) %></span> min read
    <% } %>
```

10. Save the file and close it – switch back to your Node.js terminal session, and
    run this command:

```
hexo clean && hexo generate && hexo server -no-optional
```

11. If all is well, you should see your blog appear (if not, browse to `http://`
    `localhost:4000`). Click any post heading – you will see the addition of the
    time below the main post title (as shown in Figure 6-1).

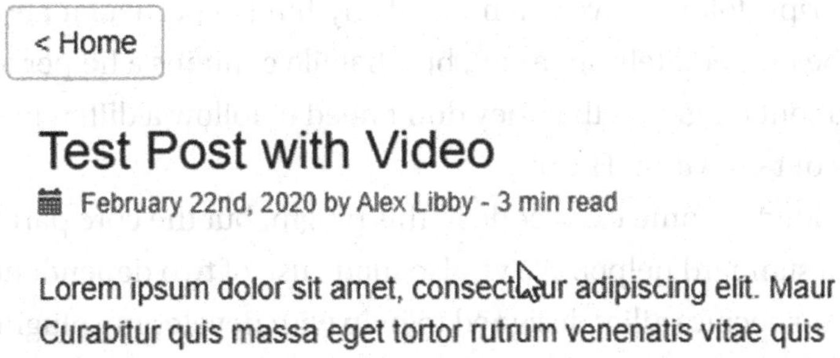

> \< Home
>
> ## Test Post with Video
> 📅 February 22nd, 2020 by Alex Libby - 3 min read
>
> Lorem ipsum dolor sit amet, consectetur adipiscing elit. Maur
> Curabitur quis massa eget tortor rutrum venenatis vitae quis

Figure 6-1. Our hexo-helper-minread plugin in operation

This plugin is an excellent example of how, with very little code, we can create
something that adds a useful function across all of our blog pages. I'm personally not
sure how helpful it is, though, as we all read at different speeds; that said, we can adjust
the value to suit!

That aside, this plugin highlights a few key points that we should be aware of, so let's
take a moment to digest what we've created in more detail.

Dissecting the code

Although we've already made use of some plugins (and created a Sass-based one in the previous chapter), an essential part of Hexo is learning how to create plugins. There will be countless instances where we find ourselves repeating code in the same blog or across multiple sites; using a plugin can help save time and effort when developing a blog. With this in mind, let's explore what we've just covered in our last exercise in more detail.

We started by creating a folder to house our plugin, within the node_modules folder; into this, we added a package.json file, created using the npm init command.

Next up, we then started to add in code for our plugin – this began with some variable declarations, before including a function to get the length() of our post text (without spaces or special characters). We then included our helper, which calculated the time taken by dividing the len() of this text by the average reading word count for English, before adding a call to display the results from within the post.ejs file.

The code for this plugin is very straightforward, but there are a couple of things to note – take a look back at the googlefonts.js file we created as a helper. It's in the themes/coffee/scripts folder. Have you noticed anything in particular about the format?

It might not be immediately apparent, but that file contains a helper too – one of the great things about plugins is that they don't need to follow a different structure to standard helpers or tags within Hexo!

Sure, we've added in some extra code in this plugin, but the core part uses the same helper syntax as a standard helper. We've also made use of two dependency plugins, one of which is a Hexo-specific utility designed to help with developing plugins. It's a small part of our plugin, but learning about these utility plugins is worth it as they can help with plugin development!

Implementing the WebP format as a plugin

For our second demo, we're going to work on a more involved plugin that adds in support for the WebP image format. "WebP?" I hear you ask. What is that, and when it's at home?

Well, you can be forgiven for wondering – it hasn't had the recognition it should have, but as an image format, WebP is not something we should ignore! Take, for example, the cruise boat image we used in previous demos – the PNG weighs in at a knockout 439 KB, yet the WebP format is a lightweight 47 KB in comparison (Figure 6-2).

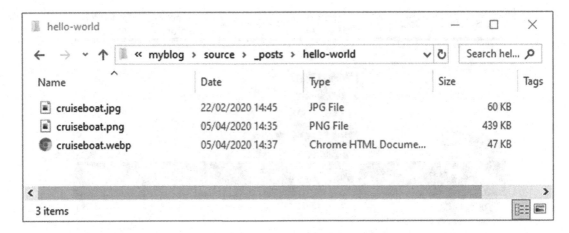

Figure 6-2. *Comparing different file sizes*

Okay, the new image file you see in Figure 6-2 was set at 90% quality, but that's nowhere near the size of the PNG file. See what I mean? Figure 6-3 shows that support for this format is excellent at present – the only two browsers that don't offer support at present are IE (no surprise there!) and Safari (although they are experimenting with support).

IE	Edge	Firefox	Chrome	Safari	Opera
			4-8		10.1
			[1] 9-22		[1] 11.5
	12-17	2-64	[2] 23-31		[2] 12.1-18
6-10	18-79	65-73	32-79	3.1-12.1	19-65
11	80	74	80	13	66
		75-76	81-83	13.1-TP	

Figure 6-3. *Desktop support for the WebP image formatSource: caniuse.com*

Support for this format is equally as good on mobile devices too. Figure 6-4 (overleaf) shows that iOS Safari is the only mainstream mobile browser not to offer support; all other mainstream mobile devices show full support for the format.

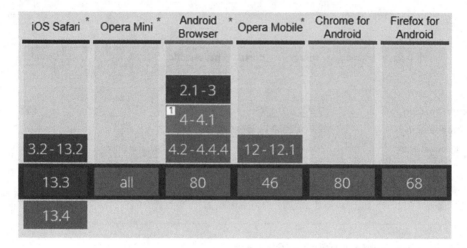

iOS Safari *	Opera Mini *	Android * Browser	Opera Mobile*	Chrome for Android	Firefox for Android
		2.1-3			
		[1] 4-4.1			
3.2-13.2		4.2-4.4.4	12-12.1		
13.3	all	80	46	80	68
13.4					

Figure 6-4. *Support for the WebP format on mobile devicesSource: caniuse.com*

Support even extends to some of the lesser-known browsers too, so there is no excuse for not using this format!

The inspiration for this plugin came from an excellent article by Jeremy Wagner on the CSS-Tricks website, at `https://css-tricks.com/using-webp-images/`. We'll make use of the ImageMin plugin for Node.js from `https://www.npmjs.com/package/imagemin-keep-folder` (with the additional support for WebP), as the basis for our plugin; we'll create it as a tag plugin, as this works best for picking up the type of change we need to make to our content.

Okay, with that in mind, let's dive in and take a look at what we're going to develop in more detail.

Building our plugin

Constructing a Hexo plugin is a straightforward process – we've already seen that they have a low barrier to entry in terms of requirements. It makes it very flexible for us to develop anything that could be useful in a Hexo environment; we're only limited by our imagination and whether we can use existing plugins to provide functionality or have to create something from the ground up!

In terms of developing our plugin, there are several tasks our plugin must incorporate, in this order:

1. Receive the name of the target image, and pass in as one of the arguments to our plugin.

2. Work out the location of where the image is.

3. Set the destination folder to be the same as the source folder.

4. Convert a copy of the image to WebP format.

5. Insert a <picture> tag with source names pointing to both the WebP format for browsers that support it and PNG as a fallback for those that don't.

6. Render the constructed HTML on-screen within our post.

Throughout this chapter, we will run through the entire development process, from constructing the code through to testing and final deployment on a live Git site, with appropriate documentation. The plugin won't be perfect, but it should give us a good ground for fine-tuning and developing it further for future use.

Okay, I've spent far too long talking (although it's all necessary) – it's time we got stuck into our code! Granted, it won't immediately show if it is a WebP format, but you'll have to take my word that it is – at least for now! Let's make a start on our exercise.

CREATING OUR PLUGIN: INSTALLING THE DEPENDENCIES

To see how we can make use of the WebP format when including images, make sure you stop your Hexo server, and then follow these steps:

1. First, go ahead and create a new folder in the node_modules folder at the root of the blog folder – call it hexo-tag-webp.

2. Next, crack open a Node.js terminal session and enter npm init -y at the prompt and press Enter to generate a package.json file (a standard requirement for all Hexo plugins).

3. Once generated, enter this command at the prompt, to install some ancillary plugins that we will use in our demo:

```
npm install imagemin-keep-folder image-webp path
```

I would **not** recommend doing this step any later unless necessary – Node.js will remove any folder from the node_modules folder that it can't locate an equivalent in the NPM registry. Take a copy of the plugin folder regularly as a backup.

4. Keep the terminal session open, but minimized – we will use it at the end of the demo.

At this point, we've done the groundwork for our demo – the next stages will work through setting up the code to make our plugin operate. We have a fair few to cover, so feel free to pause for a moment before continuing with these steps.

CREATING OUR PLUGIN: THE CODE

1. We now need to set up our plugin, so fire up your text editor; then in a new file, add in the following code which we will do block by block, starting with some variable declarations:

```
'use strict';
const imagemin = require("imagemin-keep-folder");
const webp = require("imagemin-webp");
const path = require('path');
const webpconfig = hexo.config.webpconfig;

let newfile;
```

2. The next section is the hexo extend method to initialize our new tag:

```
hexo.extend.tag.register('webp', function(args){

...INSERT HERE...
});
```

All of the following blocks should be added inside this hexo.extend method, leaving a line blank after each one, unless specified otherwise.

3. Inside of the hexo.extend block, leave a line, and then replace the
    ...INSERT HERE... with these declarations:

```
var webpSettings = {
  quality: 90,
  height: 200,
  width: 0
}
```

4. Our plugin will have a configuration section, which we will set in the
    _config.yml file; for these settings to take effect, we need to add in a
    condition to check for the presence of this configuration block and apply the
    settings if found:

```
if (hexo.config.webpconfig) {
  webpSettings = {
    quality: (hexo.config.webpconfig.quality),
    height: (hexo.config.webpconfig.height),
    width: (hexo.config.webpconfig.width)
  }
}
```

5. We now come to the core part of our plugin – leave a line, and then add in this block:

```
imagemin(['./source/**/*.png'], {
  plugins: [
    webp({
      quality: webpSettings.quality,
      resize: {
        width: webpSettings.width,
        height: webpSettings.height
      }
    })
  ]
}).then(() => {
  console.log('Images optimized');
});
```

6. We're almost done – this next section takes the value of the targeted image file
    and converts the name to the WebP equivalent:

```
newfile = path.parse(args[0]);
newfile = newfile.name + '.webp';
console.log("New file: ", newfile);
```

7. We now need to render the results of our change on-screen, which we will do
    using the <picture> tag:

```
return `
  <picture src="${newfile}" type="image/webp">
    <source srcset="${newfile}" type="image/webp">
    <img src=${args[0]} alt=${args[1]} />
  </picture>
  <div class="subtitle">${args[1]}</div>
`;
```

8. Go ahead and save the file as index.js at the root of the node_modules folder.

9. Next, switch to your root _config.yml file, and scroll to the bottom – leave a
    line blank, and then add in this configuration block:

```
# WebP config settings:
webpconfig:
  quality: 90
  height: 260
  width: 0
```

10. Save the file and close it – we don't need it again in this demo.

11. We have the basics of our plugin in place, but need to insert a call to activate
     it – crack open one of your existing post markdown files. For this demo, I will
     use the "Hello World" one that is the first post. Add in the highlighted code:

```
hexojs/hexo/issues).
```

```
<!-- more -->
```

{%- webp cruiseboat.png 'Cruise boat on river in Prague' %}

```
## Quick Start
```

12. Save the file, and then switch back to your terminal session.

13. Run this command at the prompt, to regenerate our files and restart the server:

    hexo clean && hexo generate && hexo server

14. If all is well, you will see Hexo regenerate our files – this includes a console.
    log statement to confirm that the regeneration process included our picture
    (Figure 6-5).

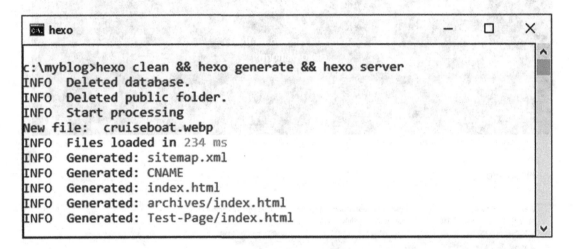

Figure 6-5. *Hexo processing pages on restart*

15. If we refresh the browser window (or browse back to http://localhost:4000),
    we will see our image appear in the "Hello World." A closer look in the console
    area will show that the <picture> tag was added, as indicated in Figure 6-6
    (overleaf).

```
▼<picture src="cruiseboat.webp" type="image/webp">
   <source srcset="cruiseboat.webp" type="image/webp">
   <img src="cruiseboat.png" alt="Cruise" boat on river in prague>
  </picture>
  <div class="subtitle">Cruise boat on river in Prague</div>
```

Figure 6-6. *Proof that our plugin added the <picture> tag*

To give you a flavor of what it will look like when we've completed our code, take a peek at Figure 6-7, to see an image present in a post, along with a suitable caption.

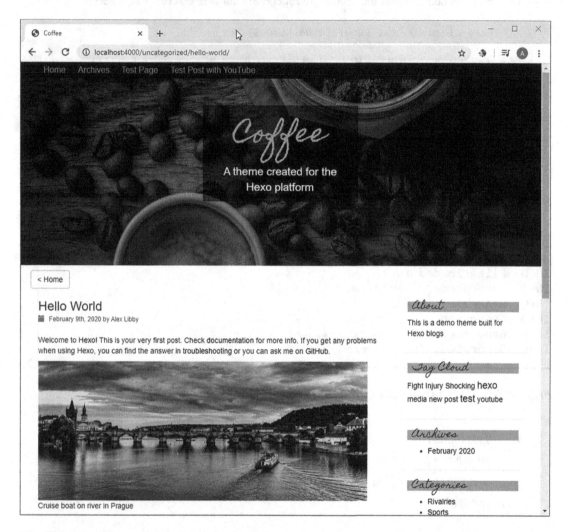

Figure 6-7. *The results of our WebP plugin*

Try running the same demo page in IE11 – this browser doesn't support the `<picture>` tag so that the PNG equivalent will be displayed instead.

Although this seemed like a lengthy exercise, some of the steps are standard fare for NPM-based plugins, so you may already be familiar with processes such as installing plugins. Nevertheless, this exercise highlights a few useful pointers around creating plugins, so let's pause for a moment to review the code we created.

Understanding the code

We started by creating a folder within the node_modules folder, as a home for our plugin – into this, we created a `package.json` file, which is standard fare for all NPM-based plugins. Our plugin makes use of several dependencies, namely, `imagemin-keep-folder`, `path,` and `imagemin`; the next task was to install each of these into our node_modules folder and add their names as dependencies to the `package.json` file.

We then began to add in the code that would form our plugin – this started with several variable declarations, followed by setting default configuration values using the `webpSettings` object. We then did a check to see if the config entries existed in the `_config.yml` file (using `hexo.config.webpconfig`) – assuming they did, we then adjusted the values accordingly.

Next up came the core part of our plugin – this took the image name passed in via the call to our plugin and created a WebP format version of it. Notice how we **didn't** specify a location for it – we assume (for now) that as we set the `post_asset_folder` value to true in our `_config.yml` file, images will be taken from there automatically. We then took the file name passed into our plugin and altered it to reference the WebP version, before rendering out the HTML5 `<picture>` tag. The final steps were to add appropriate config values into our `_config.yml` file before editing one of our posts to include the new image and regenerating the files to reflect the updated content.

Okay, let's move on. We've created our plugin and set up one of our posts to test it works; what about getting it published? Scary as that might seem (yes, others will get to see our work!), but it's not a complicated process; let's take a look at what's involved in more detail.

Publishing our plugins online

Up until now, we've created our plugin and tested it – what if we could make it available for others to use? Hexo is open source software, so it's only right we should at least consider doing so; assuming your code doesn't contain commercially sensitive details, then there is no excuse not to publish it online!

I've done this with the hexo-tag-webp plugin that we've created in this chapter – you can see the results live at `https://github.com/alexlibby/hexo-tag-webp`. There is scope for us to do more with adding features as part of developing this plugin, but we at least have a basis for others to try out!

With that in mind, let's work through the steps required to publish the plugin. This book isn't about using GitHub, so I will keep the tasks relatively high level for now, but there is plenty of documentation available online to help with some of the finer points of working with Git.

UPLOADING TO GITHUB

Let's work through the steps I went through to publish this plugin:

1. First, I made changes to the package.json file – the original `npm init -y` command serves a purpose, but it misses out some essential entries we need to add in:

   • Removed the scripts entry – it's not required

   • Added a repository section, with links to the download

   • Added a description, bugs section, keywords block, and contact details

   • Updated the dependencies

2. I then created a new repository – I used my existing development area on GitHub and created a new space at `https://github.com/alexlibby/hexo-tag-webp/`.

3. Next up, I installed GitHub Desktop – I'm a fan of using GUI-based tools if I can, and GitHub Desktop makes it easy to manage code commits.

4. I then uploaded the code files to the repository – I made a few tweaks around the license, added a readme file, and set a simple version label using the Shield service at `https://img.shields.io/`.

5. Everything is now in place – if we browse to `https://github.com/alexlibby/hexo-tag-webp/`, Figure 6-8 shows a screenshot of the newly created site on GitHub.

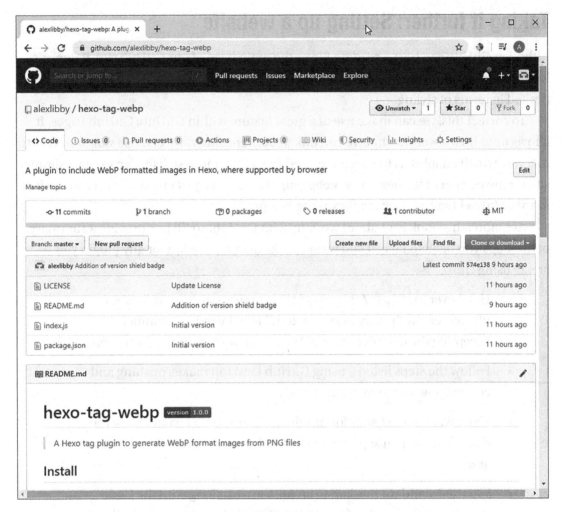

Figure 6-8. *The freshly created GitHub area for the plugin*

Once we've gotten our plugin into a decent state, then we can publish it on the main Hexo website – details on how are available at `https://hexo.io/docs/plugins#Publishing`.

Okay, we've created our plugin and made a version of it available on GitHub. A nice touch would be to provide a simple documentation site on GitHub, right? Fortunately, this is easy to do. Let's take a look at the steps involved in more detail.

Taking it further: Setting up a website

Although GitHub can host a readme file as the main page of our GitHub site, it doesn't look that great – it serves a purpose, but as we're using Markdown, it can be a little limited in terms of styling.

To correct this, we can make use of a great feature within GitHub: GitHub Pages. It allows us to host a website that we can link to our repository; we can use standard HTML markup, which enables us to provide something a little more stylish. I've set up a simple site for my version of the `hexo-tag-webp` plugin that we've just created – you can see it at `https://alexlibby.github.io/hexo-tag-webp/`.

As before, this book isn't about working with GitHub, so I'll just provide a summary of the steps you need to take, if you want to host documentation for any plugin you create using Hexo:

- Head over to `https://pages.github.com/` to start – scroll down till you see the "Ready to get started?" text. I would recommend accepting the default option of User or organization site for this one.

- Follow the steps listed – using GitHub Desktop makes pushing and committing merge requests a cinch.

- If you want to host sites for multiple plugins, then I would store the documentation in separate folders at the root of your GitHub Pages area.

- I've used standard markup to create the site, along with the Code Prettify script available from `https://github.com/google/code-prettify/`; this is great for styling the code extracts.

- If you want to customize the experience, you can even add a custom domain to your GitHub site – details on how are available at `https://help.github.com/en/github/working-with-github-pages/managing-a-custom-domain-for-your-github-pages-site#configuring-an-apex-domain`.

After a little work, we should end up with something akin to the screenshot shown in Figure 6-9.

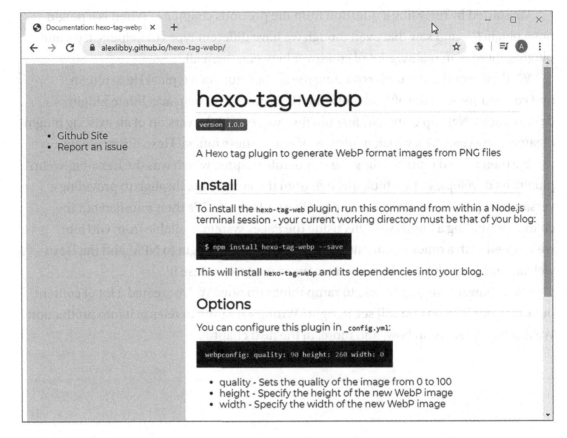

Figure 6-9. *The completed documentation site on GitHub*

The real test will come if we decide to push our plugin up to the NPM directory or add it to the plugin listing on the Hexo website – you can find details on how to do the latter at https://hexo.io/docs/plugins#Publishing, although we want to make sure we're ready to do so before submitting it!

Summary

Throughout this book thus far, we've built a theme for our blog – we could have stopped there, but that would be missing out on a critical feature: plugins! Plugins open a world of possibilities in Hexo. There are only two things that limit us: our imagination and – of course – our requirements! We've covered some essential tips and pointers when building plugins in this chapter, so let's pause for a moment to review what we've learned.

We started by revisiting a question from the previous chapter – "When is a plugin not a plugin?" – and saw that even though we have different types of helpers, tags, and plugins, there is, in reality, a lot of crossover between them all.

We then moved onto understanding the architecture of a typical Hexo plugin and covered some of the official tools that Hexo provide to help accelerate plugin development. Next up came our first plugin – we recrafted a version of an existing plugin created a few years ago, which made use of one of these official Hexo utility plugins.

We then moved onto building the star of this chapter, which was the hexo-tag-webp plugin; its development we took through from the ground up, through to providing a version that people can download from a live GitHub site. We then rounded out the chapter by adding a bonus website, using the Pages system available from GitHub; we finished with a quick comment about publishing the plugin to NPM and the Hexo website, although this would come once we're ready to release it!

Okay, onward we go. It's time to ramp things up now! We've created a lot of content, but unfortunately, no one will see it, right? Wrong – it's time to release it into production. We'll cover the steps on how, and more, in the next chapter.

CHAPTER 7

Deployment and Publishing

We've gotten everything in place – we've written our test content, we've set up our chosen theme, and we've prepared our media. But how do we get it all published?

No problem – Hexo makes deployment and publication straightforward, although there are still a few steps involved to get content online. To help with this, we can set up an automated system to upload to GitHub or GitLab and then deploy to any one of several different hosts, such as Netlify, Heroku, or even AWS! Throughout this chapter, we'll take a look at the deployment process, so you can see how we can make our content live.

Understanding the deployment process

As I am sure someone once said, we have to start somewhere – there is no better place than with understanding what is involved with deploying any Hexo project online!

There are indeed several steps involved, but nothing particularly challenging; the initial deployment will take a while to complete, but this will get quicker once we automate the deployment process (more on this later in this chapter).

To get a feel for what is involved, the first thing we should do is go through a summary of the steps required to get content from your local machine online. In summary, they are as follows:

- A tidy-up – Yes, our code might be in a half-decent state already, but there are a few things that can trip up if we're not careful; it's worth checking before pushing any changes online.

© Alex Libby 2020
A. Libby, *Practical Hexo*, https://doi.org/10.1007/978-1-4842-6089-0_7

- Create a repository – You may already have an area online on GitHub or similar; we need to have somewhere to host, and as Hexo supports automatic deployment, it makes sense to choose a host that supports automatic deployment.

- Upload files – Yes, this is the crucial part! Not everything needs to go up, so we'll cover off what should be uploaded and what must remain on your PC.

- Add Travis CI for build process – This is needed to help build a public version of your site, once it is online; it's something we need to configure, which will include uploading a .travis.yml configuration file.

- Test our site – Clearly an essential task to make sure all is good!

It might not seem a lot, but each task will have several jobs we have to do. Throughout this chapter, we're going to work through the various steps required to get our content online, so that by the end of the chapter, you will have a fully functional site that anyone can see when browsing the Web.

Okay, let's make a start. The first task we have to complete is to tidy up our content, ready for deployment.

Tidying up our content

"Tidy up?" I hear you ask. Yes, it might sound crazy, but if we don't, then it can easily trip us up! Let me explain what I mean:

- In the last two chapters, we created a handful of plugins that sat in the node_modules folder. We didn't publish them, so any time we install something, NPM will delete them. At the same time, the build process for Hexo will fail, once we've uploaded our files online. The safest way forward is to remove the folders from the `node_modules` folder and store them elsewhere for now.

- We need to change the base URL for our blog before we upload it to our host – `https://localhost:4000` will work, but it makes sense to put the right name, particularly if we have any plugins that rely on having the correct URL!

- Once we've moved our plugins out of the way, we need to change any references for webp (from the hexo-tag-webp plugin we created) to a standard link for images, so Hexo imports visual media correctly.

- It's not entirely necessary, but it's good practice also to remove any redundant themes.

Let's put this plan into action as part of the first exercise for this chapter. Before we make a start, though, there is a catch we need to be aware of: one of the changes we need to make will depend on what username you decide to use on GitHub (see part 2 of this exercise). It may or may not be available; you may find you have to repeat steps 1–3 of this exercise if you have to use an alternative username! Don't worry if this doesn't quite make sense just yet – bear with me, and I will explain all during this exercise.

PART 1: "TIDYING UP" CHANGES

To get our content tidied up, work through these steps – all of the changes will be in the myblog folder:

1. The first change is to the base URL – we need to swap it from `http://localhost:4000` to the one we will use on our GitHub site.

2. Go ahead and crack open your `_config.yml` file, then scroll down to the url: entry, and change it to `https://username.github.io` – username is the username that you will choose when you create your GitHub account. In my case, I've chosen `https://hexodemosite.github.io`, so your name will need to follow a similar format.

At this point, you may want to skip over to the "Part 2: *Uploading to GitHub*" exercise in the next section and complete up to step 10, to be sure you can create an account and repository with your chosen name. If it isn't available, then you will need to swap out what you've added in step 2 for the name that you want to use.

Assuming it's all OK, let's continue with the remaining steps:

3. We now need to move the plugins we've created in this book – while it is a shame, NPM has a nasty habit of deleting plugins that it can't find in its central repository, and we don't want to lose our work! You will need to move the `hexo-tag-webp` and `hexo-renderer-dart-sass` plugin folders from the `node_modules` folder to a folder of your choice for safekeeping.

4. Once we've moved the folders, revert to the `_config.yml` file we had open in step 2, and scroll down to the `plugins:` section.

5. From the plugins: section, remove `hexo-tag-webp` (and `hexo-renderer-dart-sass` if you have it) from here – the only plugin should be as indicated in Figure 7-1.

```
93    # Extensions
94    ## Plugins: https://hexo.io/plugins/
95    ## Themes: https://hexo.io/themes/
96    theme: coffee
97    plugins:
98        hexo-generator-cname
99        hexo-tag-webp
100
```

Figure 7-1. *Removing plugin references from _config.yml*

6. Staying in the `_config.yml` file, scroll down to the bottom and locate the section marked `#WebP config settings:` – remove this line and the next four, so the settings entries are no longer present in the file. Save the file and close it.

7. We now need to remove a little more – this time from the `post.ejs` file in our theme folder. Navigate to `themes/coffee/layout`, and then open up `post.ejs`.

8. Locate this piece of code, and remove the highlighted line:

```
<% if(page.author) { %>
    by <%- page.author %>
    - <span class="post-count"><%- minread(page.content)
    %></span> min read
  <% } %>
```

9. The next change is to update our markdown files in the sources/_posts (and the _pages folder too, if you've changed any there). For any instances where you've inserted webp (to call our new hexo-tag-webp plugin), change them to use the standard asset_img tag instead, as shown in this example:

```
<!-- more -->

{%- asset_img cruiseboat.png 'Cruise boat on river in Prague' %}

## Quick Start
```

Make sure you save and close each file as you make changes to them!

10. The final change is to remove redundant themes – this isn't strictly necessary, but having extra content present serves no benefit. Navigate to the `themes` folder, and move all **except the coffee folder** into an area for safekeeping.

There is an excellent reason for doing these final checks and tidying up now – they can potentially cause our build process to fail. This process runs through a set of tasks, which could fall over if Hexo comes across any issue with our content, such as references to plugins it can't find or plugins not yet published. The aim of completing these steps is to reduce the risk of failure. Other things may get in the way, but at least we can deal with some easy wins!

Okay, our content is now in a decent place, so we can move on with our next task: choosing our host. There are several hosts available that support Hexo, so let's take a look at some of the choices available in more detail.

Choosing a host

Choices, choices... I wonder where does one start. For some of you, it might be easy: work requirements or existing arrangements may make it easy for you.

For those of you who don't, then there are several providers we can choose from; the following list are ones which are supported by Hexo, or for which people have written plugins to help with the deployment process:

- GitLab – `https://www.gitlab.com`
- GitHub – `https://pages.github.com`
- Netlify – `https://www.netlify.com/`
- Amazon S3/CloudFront – `https://aws.amazon.com/cloudfront/`
- Heroku – `https://www.heroku.com/`
- Zeit Now – `https://zeit.co/home`

All of these use similar techniques to deploy code manually or via an automatic deployment process – in many cases, though, we need to make use of a code repository such as GitHub or GitLab to store the source code before building a release version.

To keep things simple for this chapter (and book), I've elected to go with GitHub, for several reasons:

- I already have several repositories with them and didn't want to introduce yet another provider into the mix.

- GitHub is one of two providers which are supported/recognized by Hexo.

- We also have a Hexo plugin to help with automating the deployment process (more on this later in this chapter).

Now that we've chosen our host, it is time – yes, indeed, it is time – to upload our content! There are a few steps involved in getting our content online, so to make it easier, I will split this into a four-part exercise, with convenient breaks in between to take stock of what we complete in each activity. Let's make a start with the first exercise, which is to get our content into GitHub.

Uploading content

The second of our four-part walk-through is relatively straightforward – we need to set up a hosting account and get our content uploaded. For this book, I will assume the use of GitHub; to make things easier, I would recommend setting up a new account, rather than using an existing one!

At this point, I should point out that you may prefer to use a GUI to upload content – I will assume the use of GitHub Desktop (from `https://desktop.github.com`), which will work on Windows and Mac platforms. If you prefer, you can use a different tool or the command line; please adapt the instructions as necessary.

PART 2: UPLOADING TO GITHUB

For the second of our four exercises, work through these steps:

1. We'll start by creating a new repository – for this, browse to `https://github.com`, and click Sign Up in the top right.

2. Go ahead and follow the instructions provided on-screen, including adding an email account (it's worth it!) – make sure you take note of the details you use for your account. Once done, sign in with your new account, and make sure it is validated.

3. Next, we need to create our repository – click the + sign in the top right and then New repository.

4. On the next screen, the Owner field will be your account name; enter a repository name in the format **username.github.io**, where username is your chosen username on GitHub.

5. If you want to fill in a description, then go ahead and do so – it is not compulsory for this exercise.

6. Next, choose Public as the repository type, and click the checkbox to initialize the repository with a readme file.

7. For the Add .gitignore option, choose Node, and set the Add a license to MIT.

8. Click Create repository.

9. Once done, click Clone or download and then Open GitHubDesktop.exe to clone your new repository area to your local PC.

10. Click View the files of your repository in Explorer to display the contents of your repository in Windows Explorer.

We now have our repository in place, ready for us to upload content. The next stage is to copy our site into this area – so that we can upload the content. You might want to read through these steps first, before completing each task – there are a couple of points that may catch you out.

11. Fire up (or revert to, if already open) GitHub Desktop, then click File ➤ Options, and sign in with your new account details.

12. Once signed in, click Show in Explorer to view the files stored locally – it's into this folder that we will store content.

13. Next, go ahead and copy all folders into this area, **except for the following**: /public and /node_modules.

The folder structure should be roughly similar to https://github.com/hexojs/hexo-starter, without the .gitmodules file.

---

14. Crack open the .gitignore file, and make sure it contains the following entries:

```
.DS_Store
Thumbs.db
db.json
*.log
node_modules/
public/
.deploy*/
```

15. Save the file and close it.

16. Revert back to GitHub Desktop, and then enter Initial version in the text field above the Description box (bottom left of the application window).

17. Click Commit to master and then Push origin to upload your files to your site – you now have your content ready for action!

At this point, you can minimize both GitHub Desktop and your text editor – you may need them again, just in case the build and deployment process doesn't work the first time!

Phew! You can take a breather for now: this was the most substantial part of the process! This demo was a lengthy exercise; some of the tasks though we will only need to do once (or at least per blog).

For now, though, let's pause for a moment to consider the changes we've made in this exercise in more detail – we will see why we need these changes and which ones we can skip if we're only updating existing content.

Understanding the changes

Publishing content online as part of the Hexo deployment process can seem almost as complicated as developing it! We worked through quite a few steps in this last exercise, but most of them are needed to get GitHub set up and ready for use.

We kicked off by creating a new account on GitHub for our site, before tying that to a new repository and cloning the contents to our local PC. We then moved across all of the appropriate files from the myblog folder into this area, ready for committal to GitHub. We finished the demo with a change to the gitignore file, to ensure that we exclude files and folders that we shouldn't upload to GitHub as part of the Hexo deployment process.

It's important to note that most of this exercise is only needed when we create new sites from scratch. For convenience, we built the site using a new account and repository; we could have used an existing account, but as the repository needs to be in a particular format, it makes sense to use a new one!

Okay, we still have work to do to complete our build process: the next step is to configure Travis CI to build and test our code. This step is as although we've created our source code, it's not yet in a format that allows viewing online; let's take a look at what's needed to get our site built and tested for viewing.

Testing our code with Travis CI

At this stage, we've uploaded our content and configured GitHub Pages, but our content isn't yet in a format that allows us to view it correctly. To get it there, we have to set up a build and test process – thankfully, Travis CI is perfect for this and can handle it automatically, once we've configured it.

The reason we need it is that it replaces the `hexo clean && hexo generate && hexo server` commands we've been running during development. There are a few steps we need to work through to configure our GitHub site to use it, so let's crack on and make a start on getting our site into a format viewable by people over the Internet.

If you would like to learn more about Travis CI once you've completed this exercise, then I would recommend visiting the documentation site, which is available at `https://docs.travis-ci.com/`.

PART 3: TESTING CODE WITH TRAVIS CI

To get Travis CI added to your GitHub account and set up to run builds, follow these steps – they are a little tricky, so you may want to read through them first, before completing them:

1. Go to `https://travis-ci.org`, and sign in with your GitHub account that you created back in part 1.

2. Click Authorize to accept the authorization of Travis CI to your account. Travis will redirect you to GitHub.

3. Let it redirect; then click Activate All Repositories Using GitHub Accounts ➤ Approve & Install.

4. On a new tab, we need to generate a new token with repo scopes – this is to allow Travis to build a production-ready version of your code. To do this, browse to `https://github.com/settings/tokens` in a new tab; then click Generate new token.

5. It may prompt you to sign in – use your GitHub password if needed.

6. On the next screen, enter "Building demo hexo site" (no quotes!) into the field; then tick the repo option (which will select all four sub-options).

7. Note down the token value – keep this safe! At the bottom of the page, click Generate token.

8. Switch back to the previous tab in your browser, and browse to this address, `https://travis-ci.org/github/<username>/<site name>/ settings`, where username is your GitHub account name and site name is the name you gave your site back in part 1 of this exercise.

9. Scroll down to the Environment Variables entry, then add GH_TOKEN as name, and paste in the token value from step 7 in this exercise. Click Add to save it.

10. Switch to your text editor; then in a new file, add the following code, saving it as `.travis.yml` in the GitHub local version of your site (**not** the myblog folder!):

```
sudo: false
language: node_js
node_js:
  - 10 # use nodejs v10 LTS
cache: npm
branches:
  only:
    - master # build master branch only
script:
  - hexo generate # generate static files
deploy:
  provider: pages
  skip-cleanup: true
  github-token: $GH_TOKEN
  keep-history: true
  target_branch: master
  on:
    branch: master
  local-dir: public
```

11. Save the file, and then revert back to GitHub Desktop. GitHub Desktop will have picked up the change; enter Initial version in the text field above the Description box (bottom left of the application window).

12. Click Commit to master and then Push origin to upload your files to your site – you now have your content ready for action!

13. Switch back to the browser window with Travis CI still running, and click Dashboard. If all is well, we should see Travis building our site; we are aiming to have a green tick, as shown in Figure 7-2.

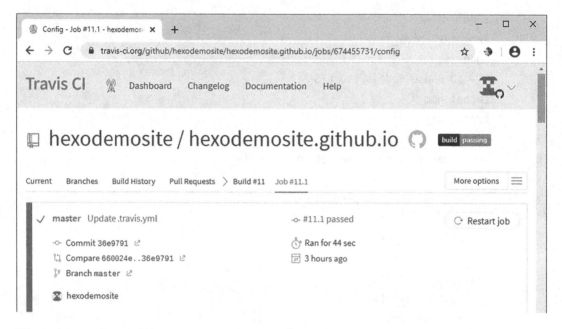

Figure 7-2. *Travis CI tests running in our browser*

14. There is one more step to work through – switch back to GitHub Desktop and try pulling down a copy of your site. You will notice it looks different; Figure 7-3 shows part of what it will look like, now that Travis has built and tested our website for us.

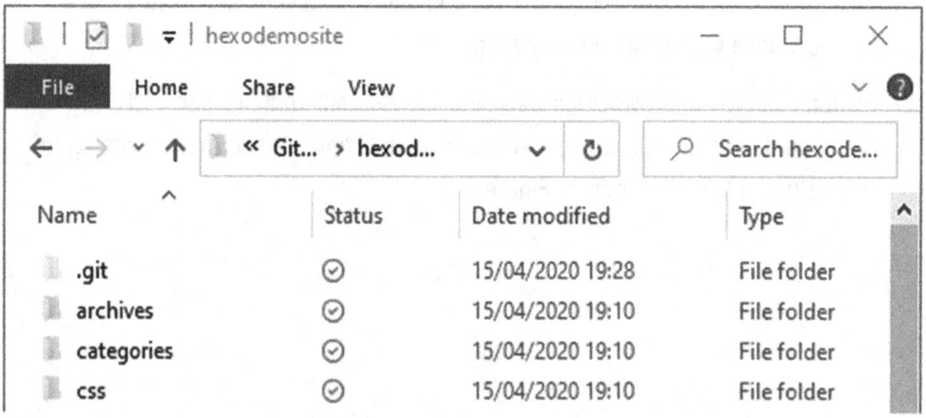

Figure 7-3. *Our newly built/compiled site, cloned to the desktop*

Okay, I confess that was still something of a more extended exercise than I had anticipated! In all truthfulness though, we won't have to complete all of these steps again for our blog; we will only have to do them if we create a new blog or need to rebuild our site from scratch.

Nevertheless, the second part of our build process shows some critical points we need to bear in mind when configuring Travis CI, so let's take a breather for a moment and review the changes made in more detail.

Breaking apart the code

Setting up Travis CI is an essential part of the build process if you are using GitHub or GitLab; you may find different methods in use on other hosts such as Netlify, although many of them are likely to be Git based! The exercise we've just completed may seem lengthy, but it's a useful way to see just what is involved in getting our content built and tested for production use.

We started by setting up an account on the Travis CI website, before tying it to (and approving access to) our GitHub Pages account. As part of this, we covered the process for generating a token that is required to allow Travis to complete the build on the GitHub site for us.

We then ran through some more configuration steps, the first being to set up an environment variable called GH_TOKEN (required for deployment), before providing more deployment settings in a Travis configuration file. The final step was to check the Travis site to confirm that it had completed a successful build of our website for us and compare what the code looks like once we've cloned it back to our PC.

Okay, let's move on. We've done the hard work, and it's time to check out the results of our efforts! It does seem like a lot of steps to go through, but many of them will be one-offs if we're building a site for the first time. I will show you a little later on how we can automate much of this process, but for now, let's sit back and enjoy the fruits of our labor.

Completing the deployment

This next exercise will seem like a walk in the park, compared to what we've had to work through thus far!

This last stage should be no more than a check that all is working as expected; if anything has gone wrong with the build process, then Travis will flag this up in the failing build request. Assuming all is good, then let's run through these last steps to complete the process of getting our site online.

PART 4: THE FINISHING STEPS

We have just a few steps to complete before we can view our website – let's work through them:

1. Once Travis CI finishes the deployment, GitHub stores the generated pages in the `master` branch of your repository – go ahead and browse to `https://github.com/<name of your repo` to view the finished results.

2. Go ahead and navigate to your site at `https://username.github.io` – you can see a screenshot of the completed deployment, which will look similar to the screenshot shown in Figure 7-4.

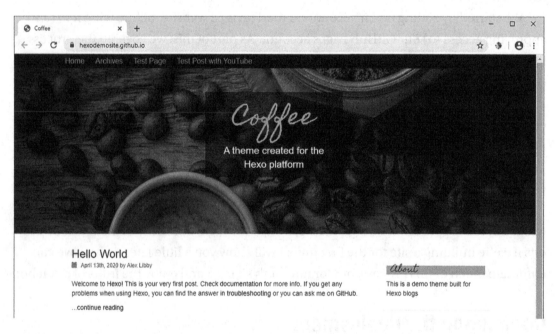

Figure 7-4. *Our site is now in production*

Our site is now online, in all its glory! It is only a start, though – a little later on, I will show you how we can assign a custom domain name to it so that to all intents and purposes, it looks like any other site on the Internet.

The best bit, though, is that hosting it on GitHub means anyone can contribute fixes or patches to improve the appearance or add new features to the site. There is so much more we can do. You can see my version online at `https://hexodemosite.github.io` – come on over to see how it should look!

If you would like more information on working with GitHub Pages and to see what features they can offer, please refer to the documentation at `https://help.github.com/categories/github-pages-basics/`.

Okay, I've talked about how we've had to complete quite a few steps to get our site online; it's time now to see how we can reduce the effort required by automating the process! Hexo can deploy content automatically to a range of different hosts, such as Git or Netlify; let's take a look at what's involved in more detail.

Automating the process

Throughout this chapter, we've explored the process for getting our content out from localhost to a live website online – we've seen how Hexo can be used with GitHub Pages to produce something that everyone can see!

Trouble is the process, as I am sure you will agree, is lengthy – can we do anything about this? Absolutely! With a little more work, we can automate the process! Critical to this is the use of the hexo-deployer-git plugin, which manages the typical Git commands that we might otherwise use to push our code up to the website.

This plugin is available from `https://github.com/hexojs/hexo-deployer-git` and can be installed in the same way as most other Hexo plugins. We'll take a more in-depth look at this plugin a little later on in this chapter.

So, assuming the plugin is installed, how would we configure Hexo to deploy to our host automatically? The core part of this process lies in the deploy: section of our `_config.yml` file, which takes this format:

```
deploy:
  type: git
  repo: <repository url>
  branch: [branch]
  message: [message]
```

We can use this method to most hosts, such as Heroku and Zeit Now (along with, of course, GitLab and GitHub). The exception to this is Netlify; this uses a GUI-based approach directly from its website.

It is worth noting that we can use a transfer mechanism as well – Hexo has details for several options such as Rsync, OpenShift, FTPSync, and SFTP, at `https://hexo.io/docs/one-command-deployment`.

Let's keep these principles in mind as we dive into our next demo – we will automate the process for uploading content to our GitHub Pages site.

DEMO: AUTOMATING THE PROCESS

To automate the process of deploying our code, we're going to use the hexo-deployer-git plugin; follow these steps to get it installed:

Note   All of these changes take place in our original `myblog` folder – not the cloned version from GitHub!

---

1. First, fire up a Node.js terminal session, and change the working directory to `myblog`.

2. At the prompt, enter this command and press Enter:

   ```
   npm install hexo-deployer-git –save
   ```

3. Once completed, go ahead and open the `_config.yml`, and then scroll to the deploy: section.

4. Alter the `deploy:` section as follows:

```
# Deployment
## Docs: https://hexo.io/docs/deployment.html
deploy:
  type: git
  repo: https://github.com/<your GitHub username>/<your GitHub site
        name>.github.io.git
  branch: master
```

5. Save the file; then switch back to the Node.js terminal session we had open in step 1.

6. At the prompt, enter this command and press Enter:

```
hexo generate --watch
```

7. We now need to create a new post to confirm our process works – in a new Node.js terminal session, and from within the `myblog` folder, enter this command and press Enter:

```
Hexo new first-post "Test Auto Deploy"
```

8. Fire up Windows Explorer (or your file manager), and check the `myblog` folder to confirm our new post has appeared (Figure 7-5).

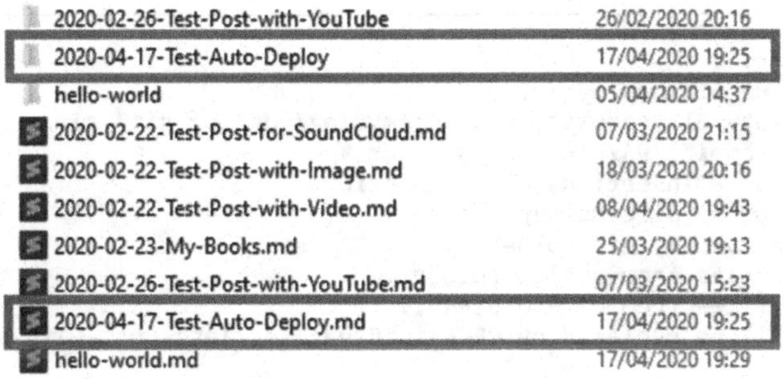

2020-02-26-Test-Post-with-YouTube	26/02/2020 20:16
2020-04-17-Test-Auto-Deploy	17/04/2020 19:25
hello-world	05/04/2020 14:37
2020-02-22-Test-Post-for-SoundCloud.md	07/03/2020 21:15
2020-02-22-Test-Post-with-Image.md	18/03/2020 20:16
2020-02-22-Test-Post-with-Video.md	08/04/2020 19:43
2020-02-23-My-Books.md	25/03/2020 19:13
2020-02-26-Test-Post-with-YouTube.md	07/03/2020 15:23
2020-04-17-Test-Auto-Deploy.md	17/04/2020 19:25
hello-world.md	17/04/2020 19:29

Figure 7-5. *Confirmation of the newly created page*

Working through these steps means we should now have an almost automated process. I said almost, as there is an instance where we have to insert our username and password for GitHub during the deploy.

The great thing though is that most of the hard work is now done automatically for us – to prove this is the case, let's run through some simple checks.

CHECKING CONTENT HAS BEEN DEPLOYED

To check changes are coming through OK, work through these tasks:

1. Fire up a Node.js terminal session, and then enter hexo clean && hexo deploy and press Enter; you should see something akin to Figure 7-6.

```
INFO  Generated: images/cruiseboat.jpg
INFO  Generated: Rivalries/Test-Post-with-Video/index.html
INFO  Generated: page/2/index.html
INFO  Generated: uncategorized/Test-Auto-Deploy/index.html
INFO  Generated: archives/2020/02/index.html
```

Figure 7-6. *...and that it has also been generated...*

2. Toward the end of this deploy process, we should see something akin to the screenshot shown in Figure 7-7.

```
INFO  42 files generated in 756 ms
INFO  Deploying: git
INFO  Setting up Git deployment...
Initialized empty Git repository in C:/myblog/.deploy_git/.git/
[master (root-commit) 9576164] First commit
 1 file changed, 0 insertions(+), 0 deletions(-)
 create mode 100644 placeholder
INFO  Clearing .deploy_git folder...
INFO  Copying files from public folder...
INFO  Copying files from extend dirs...
warning: LF will be replaced by CRLF in Rivalries/Test-Post-with-Video/index
.html.
```

Figure 7-7. *Confirmation that our code has been deployed to GitHub*

Note   The warning displayed can safely be ignored for this demo.

3. Once we've completed the previous step, GitHub will prompt you for your
    credentials – please enter them via this screen (Figure 7-8):

Figure 7-8. *GitHub login screen*

4. Once entered, you will see confirmation that our deployment is now complete,
    as indicated in Figure 7-9.

```
Node.js command prompt                                    —    □    ×
Writing objects: 100% (68/68), 17.19 MiB | 1.59 MiB/s, done.
Total 68 (delta 18), reused 0 (delta 0)
remote: Resolving deltas: 100% (18/18), done.
To https://github.com/hexodemosite/hexodemosite.github.io.git
 + 02c6fe5...d01652e HEAD -> master (forced update)
Branch 'master' set up to track remote branch 'master' from 'https://github.
com/hexodemosite/hexodemosite.github.io.git'.
[32mINFO [39m Deploy done: [35mgit[39m

c:\myblog>
```

Figure 7-9. *The automatic process is now complete*

5. Your site is now auto deployable!

Phew! A short, simple exercise. A relief to the monster demos we've just done! Automating the process is a cinch in comparison, primarily as we've already done most of the heavy lifting in the previous two exercises. Nevertheless, we should take a moment to explore the changes we've made – effected correctly – and these will dramatically help improve the time and effort needed to deploy code to production.

Understanding the changes

The process of automating the deployment process can be a real time-saver for us; provided we're only adding in posts, pages, and media, then there is no need to worry about uploading content!

To automate our deployment process, we started by installing the hexo-deployer-git plugin; this was followed by adding a handful of settings to the deploy: section of our _config.yml file. We then started the watch task runner that comes with Hexo, to keep an eye out for any changes.

Next up, we generated a test post – once we had checked that this had been generated in our local source folder, we then kicked off an instance of hexo deploy to get our content pushed up to GitHub. This we monitored via a Node.js terminal session, and once we had logged in, we could see it complete.

Let's crack on. It's time for a little theory! Okay, I promise I won't dwell on the next subject, but it's nevertheless important to learn a little about how the deployer plugin works, so we can see why it's worth the effort getting it installed for use.

Reviewing GitHub deployer

We've spent a lot of time over this chapter talking about the deployment process. I suspect in many cases you may be quite happy to use one of the existing plugins available from the plugin directory on the Hexo site.

However, if you want to create something that better fits your needs, then it's worth learning more about how deployers function at an API level. Hexo deployers all need to use a similar naming convention, much in the same way as we've seen for helpers or tags: hexo-deployer-git, in this case, the name given to the Git deployer we've used in this chapter.

They all do exactly as the name describes, and use this method:

```
hexo.extend.deployer.register(name, function(args){
  // ...

});
```

An argument `args` is passed into the function, which will contain the `deploy` values set in the `_config.yml` and the values entered by users into their terminal. If we take the hexo-deployer-git file code in more detail at https://github.com/hexojs/hexo-deployer-git/blob/master/lib/deployer.js, we can see this in use (Figure 7-10).

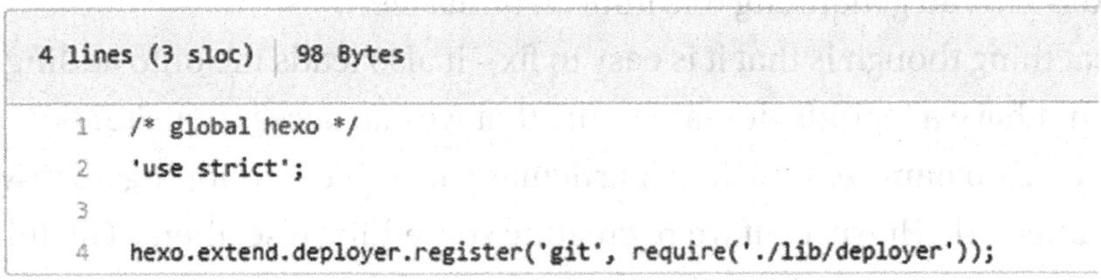

```
4 lines (3 sloc)  |  98 Bytes

1    /* global hexo */
2    'use strict';
3
4    hexo.extend.deployer.register('git', require('./lib/deployer'));
```

Figure 7-10. *Demonstrating the use of the deployer method*

If we explore the `deployer.js` file referenced in this example, we will see various functions in use; there is one of particular interest to us:

```
function push(repo) {
  return git('add', '-A').then(() => {
    return git('commit', '-m', message).catch(() => {

      // Do nothing. It's OK if nothing to commit.
    });
  }).then(() => {
    return git('push', '-u', repo.url, 'HEAD:' + repo.branch, '--force');
  });
}
```

In reality, this plugin is a front for standard commands such as `git add` or `git push` – we can, of course, use those, but having them in a plugin makes life a lot easier!

Making your content live

Remember how earlier I said you should include an email address when creating your GitHub account? Well, it was worth it for me – when I was researching content for this book, I ended up getting this email in my inbox:

> *Your CNAME file was ignored because this repository is automatically hosted from hexodemosite.github.io already. See* `https://help.github.com/articles/setting-up-your-pages-site-repository/`.

There is a good reason for getting it – we've specified a CNAME file as standard practice. However, as it has the same name as our GitHub domain, it is effectively being ignored and is instead generating this informational alert!

The great thing though is that it is easy to fix – it also leads me onto adding a bonus touch: why not have a real-life domain name that we can access our site? Some might say that the GitHub name is sufficient, particularly if you're developing a software library or a code framework. However, if we're creating something else, then a GitHub name doesn't have quite the same ring to it, does it?

Assigning a domain name

Adding a custom domain is easy when using GitHub Pages, although we do have to factor in a 24-hour delay in the process. There are several benefits though in doing this process, even though it's not specific to Hexo:

- Using a short domain name is more memorable to customers, rather than what is effectively a custom subdomain – it inspires more confidence and is better for SEO purposes.

- An external domain name can be purchased really cheaply, which makes for no excuse when it comes to creating a site.

- Having a subdomain doesn't suit every purpose – after all, why would you have a domain name such as flowers.github.com if you were a florist?

Let's take a look at the steps we need to run through to get our site set up with a custom domain in more detail.

```
PUTTING THE FINISHING TOUCHES
```

For this exercise, I will assume you have a registered domain name – it can be an existing one or one registered anew. If it is a new registration, you may want to wait 24–48 hours to allow it to propagate around DNS, before working through these steps:

1. First, browse to your GitHub site using the format `https://github.com/<name of site>`.

2. On the main page, click Settings, and then scroll down to Custom domain.

3. In the Custom domain name field, enter the name of your chosen custom domain (in my case, I used `hexodemosite.com`); then click Save. This action will create a commit that adds a CNAME file in the root of your repository.

4. Next, navigate to your DNS provider and create an A record – use the following IP addresses. You may find you need to create four separate A name records, for each of these IP addresses:

    ```
    185.199.108.153
    185.199.109.153
    185.199.110.153
    185.199.111.153
    ```

We're using A records here, as the IP addresses are known and stable; CNAME entries are name aliases that map to other names.

---

5. To confirm that your DNS record configured correctly, use the `nslookup` command – enter this in a terminal session:

    ```
    nslookup <your domain name>
    ```

If you are using Linux (or potentially Mac), then you can use this: `dig EXAMPLE.COM +noall +answer`.

It will display something similar to the screenshot shown in Figure 7-11.

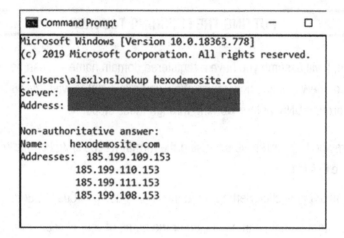

Figure 7-11. *Confirmation that DNS has updated*

6. Try browsing to your site – if all is well, we should see something akin to the
    screenshot indicated in Figure 7-12, shown overleaf.

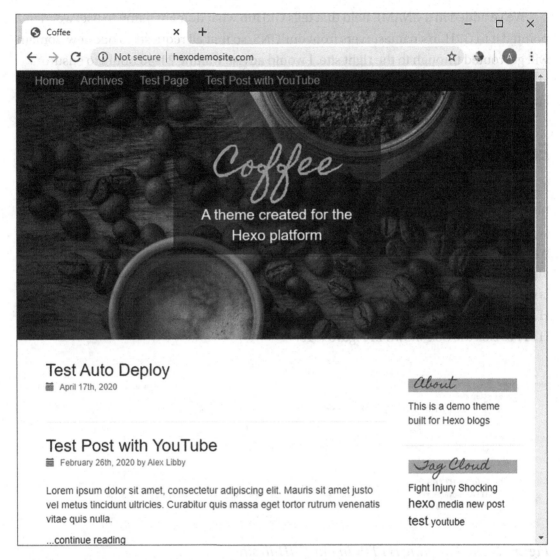

Figure 7-12. *Our completed site, under a custom domain name*

Looks great, doesn't it? Okay, it might not win any style awards, but you know what, it is now accessible under its own domain! No one (apart from you and anyone who submits a change) will be any the wiser that it's hosted on GitHub – it's just another site on the Internet...right?

We've added in a CNAME field that tells GitHub what domain name to use; we then pointed it to GitHub's nameservers from our DNS, so that all requests to our new domain will get routed through to the right site. I would advise waiting 24–48 hours to ensure DNS gets updated, but once this has happened, you have a new website set up with a custom domain name, ready for use. Or do we...?

Enforcing HTTPS encryption

Take another closer look at the screenshot in Figure 7-11 – have you noticed anything missing? You should, given insistence by a popular search engine to favor specific URLs!

I am, of course, talking about making our site secure and that it is indeed Google who gives preference to secure URLs when it comes to indexing them in its search engine. Long gone are the days where this used to be a luxury; providing a secure site is essential. Fortunately, GitHub makes this an absolute cinch to complete: to enforce HTTPS encryption for your website, navigate to the Settings page and down to Enforce HTTPS. Tick the box shown in Figure 7-13.

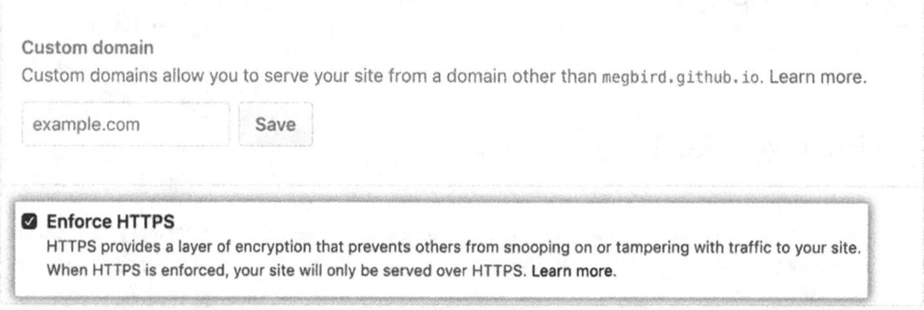

Custom domain
Custom domains allow you to serve your site from a domain other than `megbird.github.io`. Learn more.

example.com   Save

☑ **Enforce HTTPS**
HTTPS provides a layer of encryption that prevents others from snooping on or tampering with traffic to your site. When HTTPS is enforced, your site will only be served over HTTPS. **Learn more.**

Figure 7-13. *Enabling HTTPs in our GitHub site*

Here comes the 24-hour delay I mentioned earlier – it can take up to 24 hours before this option is available. If you've just added the domain name, I would suggest leaving it for 2–3 hours, at least, to allow this to take effect before you try enabling HTTPS access.

Once activated, if we browse back to the site, we should now see it available under SSL access, as indicated in Figure 7-14.

Figure 7-14. *Our secured site, under HTTPS*

It may take a few more hours for visitors further away to get updates, but there's nothing we can do about that – it's just a matter of time!

Summary

We've now reached a significant milestone – we have a fully working site that we have created and deployed from our Hexo installation, and it's working from a custom domain name to boot! We've covered some crucial points in this chapter with regard to deploying Hexo code, so let's grab a brew and take a moment to recap what we have learned.

We started by breaking down the deployment process at a high level, to understand what kind of tasks we would need to perform. We then began with the first task, before swiftly moving on to choosing our host and starting the upload process. This was followed by exploring how we can build and test our code using Travis CI, before completing the final steps of our deployment.

We then moved onto automating the process – as part of this, we explored how we might have to enter credentials, which means we can't fully automate it, but can at least reduce the steps involved. We then took a look at some of the theory behind the Deployer API, by dissecting code from the hexo-deployer-git plugin used in this chapter. We then rounded out the chapter by exploring how we can assign a custom domain name to our site, thereby removing some of the "technical" look and feel of using a GitHub domain name and making it more approachable for our customers.

Phew! We've covered a lot, but still have more to explore! At this point, we've explored all of the theory behind using Hexo; it's time to put this to good use and start creating some real-life projects! Yes, I've got a selection lined up for us to develop – in the first one, we're going to take a look at how we can improve our workflow and flesh out our blog features. Stay with me, and I will reveal how in the next chapter.

CHAPTER 8

Improving Our Workflow and Blog

Up until now, we've created our content manually and added in all of our media, again by hand. We may have touched on using a few plugins, but nothing too complicated – what we have seems to work well for our requirements.

I don't know about you, but I'm not one for resting on my laurels – I can't help but think we can do things better and improve either our workflow or what our blog offers! It's equally possible that we may find our system is already at its best. For most, though, this is unlikely, so for this chapter, we'll explore what we can add to our blog, as well as examine whether we can improve our development workflow process.

Making a start

As always, we need to start somewhere – the first task is to rename the base URL of our original blog back to `http://localhost:4000`.

Yes, you might wonder why we need to do this, but there is a simple reason – this is to give you a bit of breathing space to play with settings for each plugin locally, without disrupting what we've pushed into production. Once we've decided on the best settings and added code or styling, we can then reset the URL and deploy our changes onto the production site.

Okay, let's change the URL: this only requires a couple of steps. First, stop your blog, crack open the `_config.yml` file from the `myblog` folder, and change the `url:` entry to `url: http://localhost:4000`. That's it – once we restart, we can now deploy to our local blog again.

© Alex Libby 2020
A. Libby, *Practical Hexo*, https://doi.org/10.1007/978-1-4842-6089-0_8

Let's move on. The theme for this chapter is to experiment and have a little fun! There are dozens of ways we can improve either our blog or workflow; I've picked out a handful of projects that we will run through to augment either part of our blog. We're going to make changes to our workflow a little later, but let's first concentrate on adding features to our blog.

Making changes to our blog

If someone were to ask me how I could improve my blog, my answer would have to be "That depends." That sounds like a cop-out, but with good reason! There are dozens of different ways to add features to a Hexo blog (or indeed any blog for that matter!). Over the next few pages, I've picked out a selection of plugins or changes we can make to begin to fine-tune the user experience for our customers.

We will focus on installing them into the blog located in the `myblog` folder. If we keep to the development version, for now, it will give you a chance to experiment with each plugin's features before you install it into the live version we created in the previous chapter. With that in mind, let's take a look at what we will implement:

- We should start somewhere simple – if you've spent any time looking at the console while the blog is running, you may spot that we've had an error relating to a missing favicon! It's a little old-school, but easy to add one in – our first project will solve this issue.

- Our second project will step up things a little – how often have you made changes in code only to find you have to refresh the targeted web page manually? It's a real nuisance: why not do this automatically? No problem – this next project will kick this little irritating issue to touch.

- If you happen to run a blog that is somewhat media heavy, then you will appreciate this next project – we're going to use an old trick to lazy load images. Thankfully, there's a Hexo plugin to help with setting it up; we may not be able to see the full effects of it locally, but we can at least get it configured for use!

- The next two projects are somewhat related – since both focus on changing content associated with the front matter sections of blog posts. The first project adds in a thumbnail option into the post summary index; the second adds in a feature to allow us to display suitable description tags at the head of each blog post.

Okay, let's make a start. The first project up will be to add in a favicon to our site, so let's dive in and take a look at what's involved in more detail.

Adding a favicon

Adding a favicon to any site is a staple part of developing any website – it's something that has been around for over 20 years! It's no different for Hexo – we use the same principles when setting up a favicon, but can at the same time make use of one of its helper functions to incorporate the image.

Before we get started, you will need a suitable icon. I will assume you are using the one available from the code download; otherwise, please feel free to choose an alternative if you prefer. I would suggest keeping the same file name, though, just to keep things simple with development!

If you need to turn an image into a favicon, there are plenty of generators online: I used the one at use `https://www.favicon-generator.org`, to create the icon for this exercise.

ADDING A FAVICON

This change is an easy one to make – first make sure you've stopped your blog, before following these steps:

1. We first need to source our favicon – for this, go ahead and download the icon that's in the code download, which accompanies this book, and drop it into the root of our `myblog` folder.

2. Next, crack open your text editor and add this line to the `layout.ejs` file, within the `themes/coffee/layout` folder:

```
<link rel="icon" type="image/png" sizes="32x32" href="<%-
url_for('favicon.png') %>">
  <%- gf('Open Sans') %>
```

3. Save the file and close it. Fire up a Node.js terminal session; then change the working folder to the myblog folder.

4. At the prompt, enter this command and press Enter:

    ```
    hexo clean && hexo generate && hexo server
    ```

5. Go ahead and browse to http://localhost:4000 – if all is well, we should see our favicon appear in the browser tab…right?

Wrong. Yes, crazy as it might seem, we get…zero change. "What gives?" I hear you ask. Well, rest assured I've not done this deliberately to catch you out – trust me, it tripped me up when I first made this change! The reason for it not appearing though is simple: Chrome doesn't display the icon if the domain is not an external one (i.e., not localhost).

Don't worry though – all is not lost. To see the image appear, we have to extend that previous exercise by a few steps. As we're focusing on keeping things local for now, I will walk you through how it will appear:

- Instead of running hexo clean &&...., I ran hexo deploy, having first reset the base URL in _config.yml back to my production site.

- This action pushed the change up to my GitHub site (which you can see at https://github.com/hexodemosite/hexodemosite.github.io/blob/master/index.html); I then made sure the favicon.png file was uploaded to the root of the repository as well.

- I also had to reset the URL in my CNAME file – the upload will have reset it back to http://localhost:4000, which will fire an alert from GitHub.

- A quick check of the console log shows that Travis CI has updated the index.html file as part of its build process, as indicated in Figure 8-1.

```
<meta name="keywords" content="">
<meta name="description" content="">
<link rel="icon" type="image/png" sizes="32x32" href="/favicon.png">

    <!-- Twitter bootstrap (via cdn) -->
```

Figure 8-1. *The updated index.html file, showing our favicon link*

- A hard refresh of the browser window with Ctrl+F5 and presto! Here's the icon in all its glory (Figure 8-2):

Figure 8-2. *The updated favicon now appearing in the browser*

Hopefully, you will agree that this looks better – if only to get rid of the irritating 404 error that I am sure you will have seen in your console log area. Feel free to run through the additional changes I've made, but don't forget you will have to update your CNAME file so the code publishes correctly!

This change is a great way to show off how we can use a Hexo helper to source the image; let's take a quick look at the code changes we've made in more detail.

Breaking apart the changes

So what did we do in that last exercise? Well, the first part of it centered around sourcing an image and adding in the requisite tag to make it appear in our browser's tab.

For this, we made use of a Hexo helper, url_for() – this takes the base URL of our blog, plus any relative URL passed in as a parameter, and turns it into a full URL. We then ran the typical hexo clean commands to regenerate our content.

At this stage, we were expecting to see the icon appear; it turns out that favicons are not displayed locally. To fix it, we would need to deploy to our production site; this we could do using the setup from the previous chapter. We then walked through how to achieve this – making sure that the favicon image was at the root of our blog and that the CNAME file we used in Chapter 5 had the correct URL.

The evidence was displayed in a couple of screenshots – as these came from a live site, I would encourage you to take a look to confirm that these are indeed real and not as a result of any clever artwork!

See how easy that was? Favicons have been around for as long as I can remember – the fact that we had an error showing wouldn't have affected the overall operation of our site. But I'm one of those people who doesn't like leaving things unfixed if I can help it, so getting this plugin set up means one less error to worry about during development.

Let's move on. Next up is a pet bugbear of mine: having to refresh a screen manually after each change. Thankfully, we can automate it within a Hexo blog – it's easy to fix, although it does require another plugin...!

Refreshing the screen

So far, we've created pages and posts and added text which we've styled using Markdown syntax – we've had to refresh our browser page after every change, right?

That's a real pain – we've got better things to do! Technology is such that we can do this automatically; the best way to do this within Hexo is by use of the hexo-browsersync plugin, available from `https://www.npmjs.com/package/hexo-browsersync`. It's straightforward to install; being a Node.js-based tool, we can use the standard `npm install` approach. Let's take a look at the steps involved in getting it set up, before putting it to use as a quick test.

You may come across references to the hexo-livereload plugin; this plugin has been retired and, therefore, should not be used.

INSTALLING THE BROWSERSYNC PLUGIN

To install the browsersync plugin, follow these steps:

1. First, go ahead and stop the Hexo server in the Node.js terminal window – use Ctrl+C.

2. At the prompt, run this command, and press Enter:

    ```
    npm install -g browsersync
    ```

3. Once done, go ahead and enter this command; then press Enter:

    ```
    npm install hexo-browsersync --save
    ```

4. When the plugin installation is complete, enter hexo `server -no-optional` at the prompt; then press Enter to restart the Hexo server (the `-no-optional` is required to get around an issue with `fsevents`, which isn't supported on Windows).

5. If all is well, you will see this little message flash up in your browser when your blog is reloaded into a new window (Figure 8-3):

Figure 8-3. *Browsersync is operational*

6. You can see confirmation of when a browser window is reloaded, in the terminal session, as indicated in Figure 8-4.

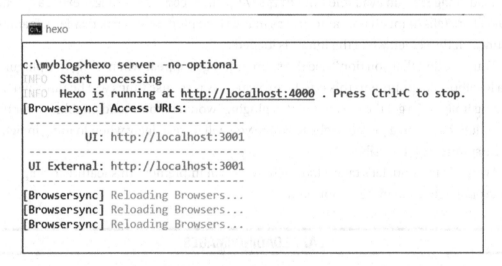

Figure 8-4. *Confirmation that our browser has reloaded the current page*

Although the installation of the browsersync password is very straightforward (and which is indeed typical of many Hexo plugins), it does highlight one crucial point. On the few occasions where you need to run the hexo `server` command, this will **not** automatically fire up a new browser session. For this, we need to add the `-no-optional` flag – a nifty little trick to help save us development time!

Okay, let's crack on. I want to show you another useful tip, this time around images. Let's say we have a media-heavy site (such as an image stock library or photographer's portfolio). Loading each image can add time to the overall page load, making it appear to run slowly, right? What can we do?

Well, one way around it is to lazy load or defer loading until the last possible moment; with the addition of a plugin and some code changes to our `_config.yml` file, this is easy to set up. Let's take a look at what's involved and what this means for us in practice.

Lazy loading images

As a concept, lazy loading images is nothing new – it's a great way to delay rendering of images until the last possible moment, thereby making pages quicker to load.

This technique is something we can easily apply to a Hexo blog, using the hexo-lazyload-image plugin available from `https://github.com/Troy-Yang/hexo-lazyload-image`. It installs in much the same way as many Hexo plugins and will display a loading spinner on the screen while the image is loaded.

You may find that you don't see the spinner images appear when using this plugin in a localhost environment; this is to be expected, as response times will be rapid when loading images. To get the best out of this plugin, I would recommend enabling it for use in production, or on a private website where you will have a delay when loading images, so the spinner will be visible.

With this in mind, let's take a look at how we can implement this feature to help make our pages even more performant.

LAZY LOADING IMAGES

To set up lazy-loaded images, run through these steps:

1. We first need to stop the Hexo server, as we're making a config change – for this, press Ctrl+C in the Node.js terminal session and press Enter when prompted.

2. Next, at the prompt, enter this command to install the lazy load plugin:

```
npm install hexo-lazyload-image --save
```

3. Once done, revert to your text editor, and open the `_config.yml` file found at the root of our blog folder.

4. Scroll down to the bottom, and add in the following code, leaving a blank line after the previous entry:

```
#Lazyloading images
lazyload:
  enable: true
  onlypost: true
  loadingImg: ../../images/loading.gif
```

5. Save the file and close it; then revert to your Node.js terminal session.

6. At the prompt, enter hexo `clean && hexo generate` to refresh our content.

7. Once done, enter hexo `server -no-optional` at the prompt and press Enter.

Your site is now ready to use the hexo-lazyload-image plugin, although you may not see loading spinners if using localhost; to get a feel for how they appear, have a look at the demo on the main page of the plugin's GitHub website.

It goes without saying that blogs need some level of visual content – yes, we can create mono-based themes that rely on icons and the like, but this makes it much harder to pull off an effective design!

If we do add in images (and this is an almost given), they must be loaded at the right point to help maintain speed – the hexo-lazyload-image plugin is perfect for this role. As we saw in the exercise we've just completed, it's a cinch to set up. Let's take a moment to consider the changes we made in more detail.

Understanding the changes

Adding the hexo-lazyload-image plugin is done in pretty much the same way as many Hexo plugins; we used a Node.js terminal session to run the standard install command to set up the plugin.

Where things differ is in how we configure it – we added a `lazyload:` configuration block into our `_config.yml` file. For convenience, we used the same values specified in the demo given on the plugin's GitHub site. For our demo, we set enable: to true to activate it; we've used the `onlypost:` `true` setting to limit exposure to just our posts (otherwise, we might see the spinner icon appear in unexpected places!). At the same time, we also specified a `loading.gif` image to be displayed when loaded.

It's worth mentioning though that lazy loading is somewhat old-school – there is indeed a newer method available that implements it natively in the browser. The developer Ben Schwarz has written a lengthy article on how to implement the "Blink LazyLoad" feature, which is being developed by Chrome and is available for all desktop browsers except IE and Safari. Support for the mobile platform isn't as good – only Chrome for Android and Android Browser support it, so a fallback plugin is still definitely needed!

For more details on this feature, please refer to the article on the CSS-Tricks website, at `https://css-tricks.com/a-native-lazy-load-for-the-web-platform/`.

Okay, let's move on. So far, we've implemented two easy plugins; it's time to switch tracks and do some editing! There are a couple of useful changes we can make to the front matter part of each blog, so let's dive in and see how we can improve on this part of the website.

Improving front matter

Over the years, I've visited hundreds of different blog sites – I've lost count of how many, although when I once did a tally of how many links I had saved, let's just say that it was about ten to twelve thousand, so I'm sure there will have been a fair few blogs bookmarked at some point!

One of the features I regularly came across was thumbnails present on the main index page of a blog site – I'm sure you will have seen the feature: something to give the front page a little visual interest and help break up the monotony of plain text. It's something worth adding to our blog, so why not take a look at how to do it?

Adding thumbnails to post summaries

Adding in thumbnails is very easy to do, although it will require a little planning – one such task is to source appropriate images! A key consideration is what image size to use – we clearly can't use something substantial, but equally, we need to strike the right balance between visual and text-based content.

In this next project, I've created an example of how we might achieve this – I've set an image size of 150px square. I would suggest using something around this size as a guideline. Let's take a look at the steps involved in more detail.

ADDING POST THUMBNAILS

To add in thumbnails, make sure you've stopped your Hexo blog, and then follow these steps:

1. The first change we need to make is to add in a thumbnail image to a selected post – we'll use this to make sure our process works. Pick a post and then open the markdown file in your text editor.

2. Just before the closing - - - in the front matter, add in this line as shown:

```
---
title: Test Post with YouTube
date: 2020-02-26 20:16:05
author: Alex Libby
tags:
thumbnail: images/cruiseboat.jpg
```

3. Save the file. Next, crack open the index.ejs file located in the themes/coffee/layout folder of the myblog project folder, and alter the code as indicated:

```
<div class='row'>
  <ul>
    <% page.posts.each(function(post){ %>
      <li>
        <% if (post.thumbnail){ %>
          <div class="post-thumbnail">
            <a href="<%- url_for(post.path) %>">
```

```
            <img src="<%- url_for(post.thumbnail) %>" alt="<%=
            post.title %>" itemprop="image">
        </a>
    </div>
    <% } %>
    <h3>
```

The code for this step (and the CSS, later) is in the accompanying code download for this book.

---

4. We now need to add in the image we want to display in our post summary index. For this, navigate to the `myblog` folder in your file manager, and then make sure you have an images folder at the root of this folder; add it in if you don't have it present.

For this demo, I've elected to use a copy of the `cruiseboat.jpg` image we used in an earlier demo.

---

5. If we were to run our demo now, we would get an image appear, but it's likely to be enormous! We need to cut it down to size, so to do this, go ahead and add the following styles to the styles.css file in the `themes/coffee/source/css` folder:

```
div.post-thumbnail {
  width: 150px;
  height: 150px;
  float: left;
  border: 1px solid pink;
  margin-right: 10px;
}

div.post-thumbnail > a > img {
  width: 150px;
  height: auto;
}
```

6. Save and close any open files, and then fire up a Node.js terminal session. Change the working folder to the `myblog` folder; then at the prompt, enter this command and press Enter:

```
hexo clean && hexo generate && hexo server
```

7. If we browse to our website at `http://localhost:4000`, we can see the addition of a thumbnail image as indicated in Figure 8-5.

Test Post with YouTube
📅 February 26th, 2020 by Alex Libby

Lorem ipsum dolor sit amet, consectetur adipiscing elit. Mauris sit amet justo vel metus tincidunt ultricies. Curabitur quis massa eget tortor rutrum venenatis vitae quis nulla.

...continue reading

Figure 8-5. Addition of a thumbnail image

This simple change adds a nice touch to the overall summary list of posts; it's also a good use of some of the API commands and Hexo API objects we can use when creating our blog. It is worth a look in more detail, so let's dive in and explore how the code operates in this exercise.

Understanding the code changes

The default Landscape theme that comes with Hexo is a good starter, but lacks a certain visual appeal – as we've seen from the exercise we've just completed, it's easy enough to add in something to brighten the post index.

This time around, we didn't have to install a plugin (which makes a change!) – instead, we added a custom variable called thumbnail into the front matter of one of our posts. Here we assigned it a link pointing to one of our images; we then added code to the `index.ejs` file that first checks for the presence of `post.thumbnail`. If this value is defined, we then add in a suitably sized image that links to the post – we use the `url_for()` helper, into which we pass `post.path`, `post.thumbnail`, and `post.title`.

On its own, this wouldn't look great, so we've added some basic styling. We can, of course, style it however we see fit, although we just need to be mindful of making sure that the size is appropriate to the location. As the last step, we ran the now-familiar hexo clean and regeneration process, before viewing the results in our browser.

Adding meta tags

This next project is a little old-school – adding in meta tags to your site. You know the ones I mean: `<meta name="description"...>` and `<meta name="keywords"...>` are just two examples that come to mind. The trouble is they are subject to abuse if we're not careful – developers have frequently stuffed meta tags with an abundance of keywords, so chances are the likes of Google will ignore them!

That aside, it's an easy change to make, so it's still worth exploring how we can implement it in Hexo – as to whether you want to use it, that decision is up to you...

ADDING META TAGS

To add in meta tags, first, stop your blog, and then follow these steps:

1. We'll start by opening the `layout.ejs` file from within the `themes/coffee` folder, in your text editor – go ahead and add in the highlighted code:

```
<!-- Use <%= page.title %> for dynamic title -->
<title><%- config.title %></title>
<meta name="keywords" content="<%= page.keywords %>">
<meta name="description" content="<%= page.description %>">
```

2. Next, we need to add in some tags to a post – go ahead and choose any post, and crack open the markdown file from within the source folder at the root of our blog folder. Just before the closing `---` of the front matter, add in these two lines:

```
thumbnail: images/cruiseboat.jpg
keywords: word1, word2, word3
description: test1, test2, test3
---
```

I chose the same post from the previous exercise, hence why you see the thumbnail entry in this example.

3. Save the files and close them – fire up a Node.js terminal session, and then change the working folder to our blog project folder.

4. At the prompt, enter this command and press Enter:

    ```
    hexo clean && hexo generate && hexo server
    ```

5. In a browser, navigate to `http://localhost:4000`, and bring up the developer console using Shift+Ctrl+I (for convenience, I'm assuming you are using Chrome). If you take a look at the Elements tab, you should see the presence of our meta tags, as indicated in Figure 8-6.

```
<meta charset="utf-8">
<!-- Use Test Post with YouTube for dynamic title -->
<title>Coffee</title>
<meta name="keywords" content="keyword1, keyword2, keyword3">
<meta name="description" content="This is a test description">
<!-- Twitter bootstrap (via cdn) -->
<link rel="stylesheet" href="https://maxcdn.bootstrapcdn.com/bo
```

Figure 8-6. *Our new meta tags present in the markup*

I'm a great fan of keeping things simple, and this second front matter change shows how we can make such a simple change that has a real benefit to the overall operation of our blog. That aside, there are some considerations we should bear in mind when implementing this feature, so let's take a look at this code a little more closely to see how it works in practice.

Exploring the changes in detail

The second, of our two front matter changes, was an equally simple change to make, but one that is a double-edged sword; use it not in the manner intended, and you are likely to feel the full effects of Google penalizing you! That said, if you were to use the Lighthouse audit facility available in Google Chrome and you haven't included the tags, that might flag up a warning too! It does feel a little like one can never win, but hey, that's web development...

Leaving aside the finer points of whether we should include the tags for a moment, the technical changes involved were minimal, so a good excuse to include them. We kicked off by adding two lines of markup into our `layout.ejs` file, which references the page object (or any instance of our blog posts). We then specified `description` and `keywords` variables in the front matter, which we reference using the `page.keywords` and `page.description` properties in our code. We finished off the demo with the usual regeneration commands before viewing the updated results in our browser.

Making changes to our workflow

Up until now, we've focused on adding features to the front end of our blog. However, what about the backend? Can we improve on this too?

The answer is yes – and in some respects, even more so. One of Hexo's dependencies is Node.js, which means we can (theoretically) make use of any one of thousands of plugins available through the NPM directory! Okay, maybe not quite as many as that, but you get the idea...

Over the next few pages, we're going to turn our focus on the backend of our blog and, in particular, how we can implement features to help with the workflow. As before, we will focus on installing them into the blog located in the `myblog` folder for now. In essence, this is to give you a chance to experiment with each plugin's features, before you install it into the live version we created in the previous chapter. With that in mind, let's take a look at what we will implement:

- The first project we're going to work on for our backend is to implement the Autolinker plugin. While this won't show anything per se, it will automatically convert any link we later add into a clickable URL.

- At some point, I suspect you will have come across the ubiquitous Autoprefixer plugin; we're going to implement it as our second project, to help with managing vendor prefixes in our styling code.

- Mention the word "SEO," and you might be forgiven for wondering what exactly we might be able to do, as SEO is such a broad topic! There is indeed a simple change we can make, though: we can add in the "noopener" or "noreferrer" tag to all links automatically, to help with security. It's a simple change to make, so why not?

Okay, let's make a start. The first project up will be to manage adding in vendor prefixes to our styling. It might be a little old-school, but we haven't yet consigned prefixes to the annals of history; anything we can do to manage them will be a real benefit to us! Let's dive in and take a look at what's involved in more detail.

Making use of Autoprefixer

Hands up how many of you find yourselves needing to add in vendor prefixes? I'll bet there will be a few of you who fall into this category – dealing with them is a real pain! Hopefully, there will be a day when we can push vendor prefixes to history, but until that day comes...

Enough with the dreaming – back to reality! To deal with vendor prefixes in Hexo, we can make use of the hexo-autoprefixer plugin (from `https://github.com/hexojs/hexo-autoprefixer`); this acts as an abstract layer to the Autoprefixer tool. There is a catch, though, with using it – I'll explore this shortly, but for now, let's get it installed and tested in our environment.

SETTING UP AUTOPREFIXER

To get Autoprefixer installed and ready for use, make sure you've first stopped your blog, and then follow these steps:

1. First, we need to install the hexo plugin for Autoprefixer – fire up a Node.js terminal session, and change the working folder to the `myblog` folder.

2. Next, at the prompt, enter this command and press Enter:

```
npm install hexo-autoprefixer --save
```

3. We need to add in some configuration options – for this, crack open your `_config.yml` file at the root of the `myblog` folder (not the one in your theme folder!). Leave a line blank at the end of the file, and then add in this code:

```
autoprefixer:
  exclude:
    - '*.min.css'
  browsers:
    - 'last 2 versions'
```

4. We need to add in something to test that Autoprefixer is working – for this, crack open the styles.css file in the themes/coffee/source/css folder, and add in the following code:

```
@keyframes slidein {
  from {
    transform: translateX(0%);
  }

  to {
    transform: translateX(100%);
  }
}
```

5. Save the file and close both it and the _config.yml file – we don't need to keep them open.

6. Switch back to the Node.js terminal session, and run this command at the prompt to regenerate our blog content:

```
hexo clean && hexo generate && hexo server
```

7. Once completed, go ahead and browse to http://localhost:4000 – if all is well, we should see no visual change, but a check in the public/css folder will reveal that Autoprefixer has indeed kicked in (Figure 8-7, shown overleaf).

```
inline-block}div.post-thumbnail{width:150px;height:150px;float:
height:auto}@-webkit-keyframes slidein{from{-webkit-transform:
translateX(0);transform:translateX(0)}to{-webkit-transform:
translateX(100%);transform:translateX(100%)}}@keyframes slidein{
from{-webkit-transform:translateX(0);transform:translateX(0)}to{
-webkit-transform:translateX(100%);transform:translateX(100%)}}
```

Figure 8-7. The results of our compiled styles.css, with vendor prefixes applied

At face value, this looks like a practical tool to have in our workflow – after all, anything we can do to automate manual tasks such as this has to be a benefit to us.

Although the changes we've made are minimal and follow similar steps to most Hexo plugins, there are a couple of points we should explore further – one of which could prove a little controversial! I'll go through that in a moment, but for now, let's take a look at the technical changes we've made in more detail.

Understanding how our code works

So, how does our plugin work? The key to the last exercise lies in this block of code that we added to our _config.yml file:

```
autoprefixer:
  exclude:
    - '*.min.css'
  browsers:
    - 'last 2 versions'
```

After installing the plugin using the (by now familiar) standard process, we added these configuration options into the _config.yml file. The two settings tell the hexo-autoprefixer plugin to exclude any files already minified and to only add in vendor prefixes for the last two versions of a browser. We then ran the standard clean and regeneration process – the plugin kicked in at this point and produced our file with the appropriate vendor prefixes included in the source.

It's worth noting that other options are available for the browsers property – you can see the full list at https://github.com/browserslist/browserslist-full-list.

Using this plugin: An epilogue

All is not well though – if you take a closer look at the compilation process, you will no doubt see the message displayed in Figure 8-8.

```
c:\myblog>hexo server
INFO  Start processing
INFO  Hexo is running at http://localhost:4000 . Press Ctrl+C to stop.

   Replace Autoprefixer browsers option to Browserslist config.
   Use browserslist key in package.json or .browserslistrc file.

   Using browsers option can cause errors. Browserslist config
   can be used for Babel, Autoprefixer, postcss-normalize and other tools.

   If you really need to use option, rename it to overrideBrowserslist.

   Learn more at:
   https://github.com/browserslist/browserslist#readme
   https://twitter.com/browserslist
```

Figure 8-8. *Autoprefixer warning message*

Ouch! That doesn't look good, does it? This warning might put some people off, but it's not as scary as it might seem. It does raise some important points though:

- If we use the browserlist configuration option as suggested, it breaks the plugin – an issue for this has been raised at `https://github.com/hexojs/hexo-autoprefixer/issues/45`, although it has yet to have any action on it, at the time of writing.

- It raises the question that if it's not likely to be fixed any time soon, do we want to see the warning? It is indeed annoying to see it, but the plugin is still performing as expected. Normally I wouldn't advocate using a tool that displayed this kind of warning, but there are very few options available. If we don't use it, then it means having to implement an alternative using something like Grunt, Gulp, or PostCSS.

There is one small good thing, though – even though we've added in that new style rule to prove it works, a closer look at the code has revealed that Autoprefixer has added prefixes to other rules as well. It turns out that we didn't need to add in that extra rule after all, but hey, even though we're not using it, it isn't doing any harm!

Okay, let's move on to our next project, and with that a question: how can you improve SEO?

Improving SEO

Ask anyone that question, and you will likely open a real can of worms, as the English phrase goes – in other words, you could open yourself to a whole heap of trouble!

Improving SEO is a vast topic, and one that is critical to the success of any company with an online presence – there is a whole heap of different tasks you can perform to help improve your search ranking. One might rightly ask what we can do in a single chapter. It's a fair question! There is a task we can perform, though, and that relates to adding rel= tags against any of our external links.

How can this help? Well, it all boils down to how search engines such as Google treat your external links. If we don't put these tags in, then we are effectively casting a vote of confidence in that page; this is not something you necessarily want to do! At the same time, Google is known for its harsh view on sites that are effectively link dumping grounds; adding rel= tags will stop it from following through on these tags and help to preserve your SEO rankings.

Fortunately, we can automate the process by using the hexo-filter-no-follow plugin – let's take a look at how in more detail.

ADDING NO-FOLLOW TAGS

To set up our plugin to automatically add in no-follow tags, make sure you stop your Hexo blog, and then follow these steps:

1. First, fire up a Node.js terminal session, and then change the working folder to the myblog folder.

2. At the prompt, enter this command and press Enter:

    ```
    npm install hexo-filter-nofollow --save
    ```

3. Next, crack open your text editor, then open the _config.yml file, and add this block in at the bottom – leave a blank line after the previous block:

    ```
    nofollow:
      enable: true
      field: site
      exclude:
        - 'exclude1.com'
        - 'exclude2.com'
    ```

4. Save the file and close it – we don't need it open for the rest of this exercise.

5. Next, open one of the markdown files for your posts, and add this code in somewhere – it doesn't matter if this is in a paragraph or at the end of the document:

    ```
    Link: www.example.com
    ```

6. Save and close the file – then revert to your Node.js terminal session from step 1.

7. At the prompt, enter this command and press Enter:

    ```
    hexo clean && hexo generate && hexo server
    ```

8. If all is well, you will see your link appear when you browse to `http://localhost:4000`, and click the link to your chosen post – Figure 8-9 shows the link in place.

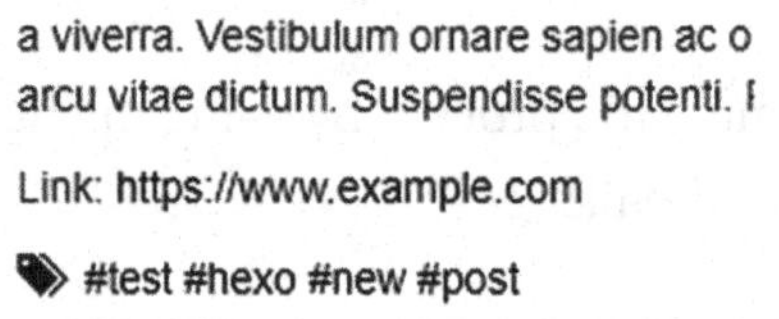

> a viverra. Vestibulum ornare sapien ac o
> arcu vitae dictum. Suspendisse potenti. F
>
> Link: https://www.example.com
>
> #test #hexo #new #post

Figure 8-9. *The link with the SEO rel tag in place*

Hold on. It looks like the plugin hasn't done anything – what gives? Well, it has done something, but the screenshot doesn't show off the effect that well! The best test is to take a peek under the covers, using your browser devtools app – Figure 8-10 shows that our plugin has done its work.

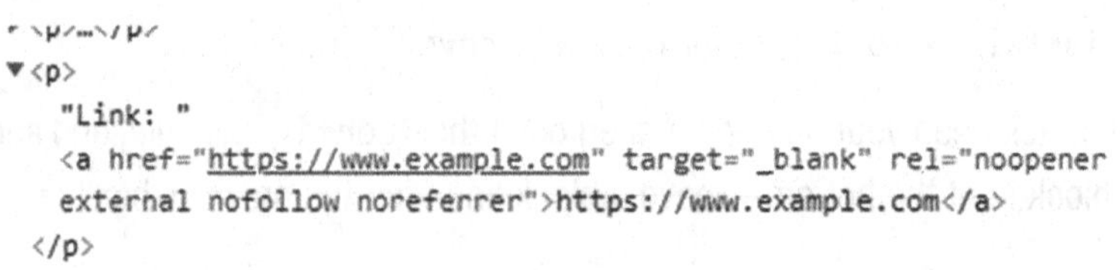

```
 ▶ <p>…</p>
 ▼ <p>
     "Link: "
     <a href="https://www.example.com" target="_blank" rel="noopener
     external nofollow noreferrer">https://www.example.com</a>
   </p>
```

Figure 8-10. *Proof that the hexo-no-follow plugin has done its job*

Although this was a simple plugin to install and configure, it does highlight a few important points we need to consider. Let's pause for a moment to explore how this plugin functions in greater detail.

Breaking apart the changes made

Now that we have the plugin installed, how does it work? Well, the crux of this demo hangs on this block of code that we added to our `_config.yml` file:

```
nofollow:
  enable: true
  field: site
  exclude:
    - 'exclude1.com'
    - 'exclude2.com'
```

Once we had installed the plugin, we added these configuration options into the `_config.yml` file. These tell the hexo-autoprefixer plugin to check the entire site for any links and that we should exclude any domains beginning with exclude1.com or exclude2.com. We then ran the standard clean and regeneration process, as before – the plugin kicked in at this point and updated all of the URLs with the appropriate rel tags throughout our blog.

Okay, let's crack on. The last project we're going to look at is implementing redirects in our blog. It is a useful technique to help minimize instances where we get the dreaded 404, or page not found, error. The plugin we will use, hexo-generator-alias, can be used to perform all manner of redirects – we might use it as a form of short URL (such as done by bit.ly) or redirect if we have to move pages around our site. Let's take a look at what is involved and what this means for us in practice.

Implementing a 404 redirect

404 – three numbers that should strike fear into any developer! Yes, this number signifies the dreaded page not found error, not something any developer wants to see on their site. Thankfully, it is easy enough to implement a redirect – I will show you how, as part of this next exercise.

REDIRECTING CONTENT

To set up our plugin to automatically redirect pages, make sure you stop your Hexo blog, and then follow these steps:

1. First, fire up a Node.js terminal session; then change the working folder to the myblog folder.

2. At the prompt, enter this command and press Enter:

   ```
   npm install hexo-generator-alias --save
   ```

3. Next, crack open your text editor, then open the _config.yml file, and add this block in at the bottom – leave a blank line after the previous block:

   ```
   alias:
     about/: /Test-page/index.html
   ```

4. Save the file and close it – we don't need it open for the rest of this exercise.

5. Switch back to a Node.js terminal session; then at the prompt, enter this command and press Enter:

   ```
   hexo clean && hexo generate && hexo server
   ```

6. If all is well, you will see your page redirect when you browse to http://localhost:4000/about/ – Figure 8-11 shows that the page has redirected.

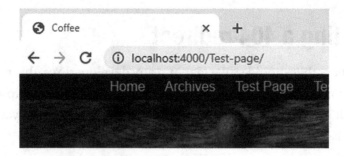

Figure 8-11. *Our redirected page has now landed*

7. Take a look at Figure 8-12 for real proof though. We can see the request for the about page; it shows a 302 or Found status, but that the next URL below it is our redirected page.

Name	Status	Type	Initiator
☐ about	302		Other
about/	200	document	:4000/about
Test-page/	304	document	Other
bootstrap.min.css	200	stylesheet	(index)
font-awesome.min.css	200	stylesheet	(index)

Figure 8-12. *Proof that our page has redirected successfully*

This change is one that should be at the top of any Hexo developer's list – granted, we shouldn't have any missing pages, but you can never be too careful! Now that it is in, let's take a quick look at how it works and the benefits of using it in practice.

Understanding the changes

This plugin has to be one of the simplest to install! It doesn't require any configuring as such – at least not in terms of setting any properties. The only configuration that we need to add is the list of URLs that need to be redirected. These we add to the `_config.yml` file, under the alias block, thus:

```
alias:
  about/: /Test-page/index.html
```

Once we've set up the list, we then ran the standard clean and regeneration process, as before – the plugin kicks in once we browse to any of the affected URLs on the left side of the list. Hexo automatically takes care of redirecting to the new URL; this the browser treats as a 302 code in the console, which means we can maintain SEO rankings as browsers treat this as a permanent redirect to a new URL. We can also use it to implement a service similar to that offered by TinyURL, where we can add in a short-form URL and get our browser to automatically redirect to a much longer URL within our blog – perfect for marketing campaigns!

187

Summary

When it comes to experimenting with Hexo, there are dozens of different plugins and code changes we can explore. The Hexo website hosts documentation on all of the API methods and objects that we can use, so we can begin to manipulate the experience offered by our blog. We've covered several useful tips and tricks in this chapter, so let's take a moment to review what we have learned in this chapter.

We kicked off by resetting the URL in our config file so that we can install plugins without affecting production; we then took a look at some of the changes we would make in this chapter. The first change began with adding the traditional favicon before we moved onto implementing the browsersync plugin to help with automatically refreshing our screen after each change.

Next up, we took a look at how to apply lazy loading for images, to help maintain speed and effective operation of our blog; we then switched to editing the front matter sections to add in two new features directly in code.

We then took a look at some of the changes we could make to the backend of our blog – the first up was to implement the Autoprefixer tool to help manage vendor prefixes. We then explored a simple change that could help with improving SEO, before rounding out with a straightforward trick to set up redirects to help prevent dreaded 404 errors from appearing in our blog.

Phew! Another whirlwind chapter comes to a close; we still have more to cover! Our next project will have something of an international feel to it; in this modern age of the Internet, customers want content in their local language, rather than having to navigate around a site in an unfamiliar tongue. Hexo is perfect for this task, so stay with me as I show you how to add an international flair to our blog in the next chapter.

## CHAPTER 9

Localizing Content

The phrase "localizing content" reminds me of the British comedy *Fawlty Towers*. In it, we see Manuel, a well-meaning but disorganized and confused waiter who is frequently verbally abused by his boss. He gets all manner of verbal abuse, to which his response is often "¿Qué?" ("What?")

Joking aside, localizing content in this age of global access via the Internet is essential – not everyone speaks the same language, and we might end up with customers giving the same response if they can't understand the content written in a language other than their own!

Fortunately, we can address this using the internationalization feature from within Hexo; we can write language files based around core content, and these will be automatically pulled in by Hexo during publication. Throughout this chapter, I will take you through the necessary steps you need to cover to add some form of language support to our blog. At the same time, we'll cover some of the points we need to consider when architecting language support – it's not just about changing labels over to your chosen language!

Setting the background

So, where does one start when it comes to localizing content in a Hexo blog?

At its core is a single value – language – which we have to set in the _config.yml file; this we can do in one of two ways:

```
# Single language used site-wide
language: fr

# Multiple languages
language:
- fr
- en
```

Although it's tempting to rush in and change it over, I would recommend taking a step back and setting up the data first. Language support takes the form of a JSON file, an excerpt of which might look like that shown in Figure 9-1.

```
1    index:
2      title: Practical Hexo | Home
3      header:
4        title: Coffee
5        description: A theme created for the Hexo platform
6      menu:
7        Home: Home
```

Figure 9-1.   *A section from a language JSON file*

Language files are just JSON files, with entries constructed in a key-value pair. If, for example, we wanted to use the word title (from line 2, in Figure 9-1), Hexo would return Practical Hexo | Home for our blog title. We can group entries – this is perfect if you have several entries that relate to the same thing, such as the header of our blog.

At first, this might not entirely make sense by itself, but it all should fall into place, once we implement the third and final part: referencing the text in our theme. Take for example this modified code, from the header.ejs file we've used in our theme:

```
<div class='row text-center'>
  <h1 class="blog-title"><%=__('index.header.title') %></h1>
  <p class="lead blog-description">
      <% if (config.subtitle){ %>
        <%= __('index.header.description') %>
    <% } %>
  </p>
</div>
```

Have you noticed anything? I've already converted this to use localized language files – in each case, we use the __('...') function, in place of hard-coded text. The three dots would be replaced by the chosen label from our YAML file. Here, our two highlighted examples will translate to the entries on lines 4 and 5 of the YAML file, as was shown in Figure 9-1.

Its' worth noting that if we need to show pluralized labels (such as "3 apples"), we can use the _p function instead – this takes a second parameter, as shown in this example: `<%= _p('fruit.apples', 3) %>`

Okay, there is more we can do with regard to automatically detecting which language Hexo should use, but for now, let's move on. It's not just a case of converting pages! There is more we need to consider: how we structure our site and what impact that might have on areas such as SEO. We'll come back to this shortly, but for now, let's take a look at sourcing and creating language files for our site.

Sourcing the data

The first step in converting our site is to create the language files that we need – these require nothing more than a text editor – which we can do while the site is still running.

For the first demo of this chapter, I will work through creating both English and French language files; we will supplement this with a right-to-left (or RTL) language in a later demo. With this in mind, let's take a look at the steps involved in more detail.

The translations I've included are from Google Translate, so I can't vouch for accuracy in this context! Each demo is purely about the technical means of translating; we should source content from appropriate sources.

SETTING UP THE DATA FILES

To create our language files, follow these steps:

1. First, we need to create a folder within your theme folder – this needs to be called languages and saved at `\themes\coffee\languages`.

2. Next, crack open your text editor, and create a new file as `en.yml` in the language folder, and add in these entries:

```
index:
  title: Practical Hexo | Home
  header:
    title: Coffee
    description: A theme created for the Hexo platform
  menu:
    Home: Home
    Archives: Archives
    Test: Test Page
    YTPage: Test Post with YouTube
  about:
    title: About
  tagcloud:
    title: Tag Cloud
  archivelist:
    title: Archives
  categories:
    title: Categories
  pagination:
    forward: Next
    backward: Previous
  navlinks:
    continue: ...continue reading
page:
  home: Home
  authored: by
```

3. In a new file, add the following, and save it as `fr.yml` in the same folder:

```
index:
  title: Practical Hexo | Acceuil
  header:
    title: Coffee
    description: Un thème créé pour la plateforme Hexo
  menu:
    Home: Acceuil
    Archives: Les Archives
```

```
    Test: Page de Test
    YTPage: Page de test YouTube
  about:
    title: A propos de
  tagcloud:
    title: Sujets populaires
  archivelist:
    title: Les Archives
  categories:
    title: Catégories
  pagination:
    forward: Prochain
    backward: Précédent
  navlinks:
    continue: ...continuez la lecture
page:
  home: Accueil
  authoredby: par
```

4. Save and close files, and close your editor – we now have our language files, ready for use in the next exercise.

A nice easy change to start with. We won't see the benefits from it immediately, but don't worry – that will change! Nevertheless, it's a crucial step in converting our site to displaying content in different languages.

With this in mind, let's pause for a moment to explore the code changes we've made in more detail and see how these fit into the broader picture of localizing content.

Breaking apart the changes

When adding language support to any blog, preparation is vital – this is no different when using Hexo. In our demo, we've created two content files – both use YAML syntax – which we store inside the languages folder of our theme.

The key to making this work is structuring each file. The files each contain all of the translated labels for a specific language: in this case, we have two – en.yml for English and fr.yml for French.

Inside each, we've grouped fields according to page type – the most prominent block relating to the index page and a few at the end for the post page type. Take a look at the index block – have you noticed how we have fields set up for areas such as `header`, `about`, and `tagcloud`? These relate directly to the same areas of the website, making it easier to keep track. There is no hard-and-fast rule about how we set up this structure, but it's important to define something that

- Accurately describes the structure (i.e., you don't want something like `index.title.title` for the page title!)

- Reduces repetition and makes sense in terms of the feature you want to add to your blog

Above all, I would recommend making sure that you have the same key-value structure in each file – labels set in a different order for each country will only make things harder to manage!

Let's move on. Now that we have our "translated" content (I say translated, as we have not verified it for accuracy), now is a perfect moment to explore the broader picture around architecting language support. There are a few things we need to consider, so let's dive in and take a look at these points in more detail.

Architecting language support

Before we get into the technical detail about configuring our blog for language support, there is one big question we must ask ourselves – just how are we going to set it up?

There is a good reason for asking this question – the strategy you decide to use will affect how you generate your content and, in some cases, where we host it. One of the co-founders of the digital marketing agency NP Digital, Neil Patel, has written an excellent article on the impact choosing a domain/language structure can have on your SEO; in summary, there are several options available:

- We can choose between either targeting a country or a specific language.

- We might choose to use subdirectories or subdomains.

- We choose to use a subdomain and subdirectory to host our content.

Neil has rated each option in terms of impact on SEO; I've summarized them in Table 9-1.

Table 9-1. *Options available when considering multiple-language support (source: neilpatel.com)*

Rating	Targeting a country	Targeting a language
Best	Use a ccTLD and subfolder such as hexoblog.es/blog/	Use a subdirectory with a TLD such as hexoblog.com/es/blog/
	Use a TLD and subdirectory such as hexoblog.com/es/	Use a subdomain such as es.hexoblog.com, along with a folder: es.hexoblog.com/blog/
Worst	Use a subdomain with or without a folder, such as es.hexoblog.com/blog/	

At first glance, there would appear to be a few options available. However, some of these options can be discounted, owing to some limitations in Hexo:

- If we create posts in multiple languages (it doesn't matter which), these are all displayed on the main index page – we're not able to alter the contents of the index.ejs file to only show those that are for a chosen language. It may not be an issue for some, but could get a little unwieldy for those who have to wade through posts of both languages to find the one they want!

- If we use a subdirectory/folder approach, we can create posts in a subfolder, according to the language specified – for example, en for English, fr for French, and so on. However, we would need index files within these areas as well, effectively to replace the main index file – the current version of Hexo makes it very difficult, if not impossible, to create them, **in the right place**! (I say difficult, as we can create posts, but Hexo appears to ignore or not support the --lang parameter used to specify in which folder when creating sub-index files.)

It effectively means that there are only two options available to us that fit the support offered by Hexo: they are to use a ccTLD (and a subfolder if desired) if we want to target on a per-country basis and, if we prefer to target on a per-language basis, to then use a subdomain and folder – as long as we don't use the latter to identify the country! Let's take a moment to understand why I've selected these two options:

- We can, by default, eliminate the worst option – it doesn't make sense to use something that is almost certainly going to be detrimental to our blog.

- Using a folder to store the country is only partially possible at present. We can create posts that sit in this folder, but Hexo will expect us to manage routing to those folders separately; this adds complexity that will seem overkill on a smaller blog. It will likely need us to create a placeholder markdown file inside each language folder, which doesn't seem to work as expected anyway!

- Although current limitations mean that we should aim to have a single language per blog for the best effect, all is not lost – there is a way to mix languages used in our posts. I will show you how later in this chapter.

With that in mind, it's time to outline the approach we're going to use in this chapter. We will focus on two techniques in particular: we'll start with providing essential support that allows for a mix of languages to be used on a per-post basis.

The next change we make will improve on this support so that we use just one language across the whole site; this will be perfect for single-language applications. The final change will cover how we can support right-to-left (or RTL) languages such as Arabic; this means we should be able to cater for most languages available worldwide.

Okay, let's resume with the practical work. The next step in doing so involves updating our theme to reference the content we've just created. Let's take a peek at how to do this, so we can understand what we should and should not change in our theme.

Adding support to the theme

This next step is probably the most important of the two steps that it takes to add in language support – we can produce language files ad infinitum, but this isn't any good if we can't use them!

Let's set that right: to do so involves the use of the __(...) function in Hexo, where we pass in a value from the YAML files we've just created that relates to a label on our website. It's an easy change to make, although we have to be careful about where we do it – I'll show you what I mean, as part of the next exercise.

ADDING LOCALIZATION SUPPORT

For this next exercise, follow these steps to add in localization support:

1. Crack open the _config.yml file in your text editor, and set the language property as indicated in Figure 9-2.

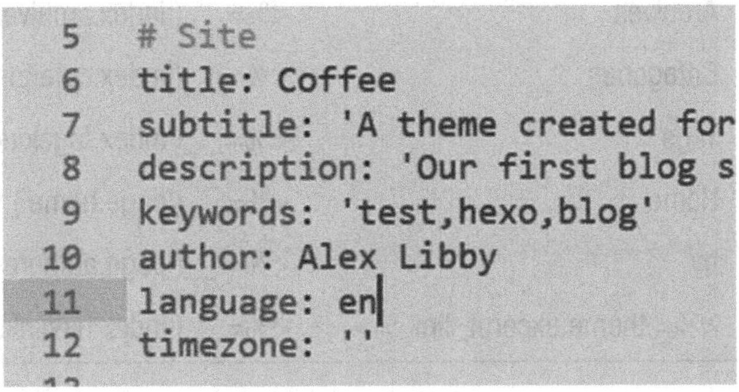

```
 5    # Site
 6    title: Coffee
 7    subtitle: 'A theme created for
 8    description: 'Our first blog s
 9    keywords: 'test,hexo,blog'
10    author: Alex Libby
11    language: en|
12    timezone: ''
```

Figure 9-2. *Extract from our _config.yml file*

You may wonder why we're using just en for the language, when you might expect en-US or en-GB. Hexo follows the ISO standard for language codes; the second part of the tag is optional. In this case, we're specifying just English and not tying it to a specific country or region such as American English.

---

2. Next, open the layout.ejs file which is in the \themes\coffee\layout folder, and modify the <html> tag at the top to <html lang="en">.

3. Next, open the header.ejs folder from the themes\coffee\layout_partial folder, and change the code as highlighted:

```
<div class='row text-center'>
  <h1 class="blog-title"><%=__('index.header.title') %></h1>
  <p class="lead blog-description">
```

4. We need to add in similar changes elsewhere in our blog – use the same principle from step 3, and change the entries in files listed in Table 9-2.

Table 9-2. *The remaining labels to change, within the layout folder*

Name of file	Change from...	To...
pagination.ejs	Next	<%= __('index.pagination.forward') %>
pagination.ejs	Previous	<%= __('index.pagination.backward') %>
about.ejs	About	<%= __('index.about.title') %>
archives.ejs	Archives	<%= __('index.archivelist.title') %>
categories.ejs	Categories	<%= __('index.categories.title') %>
tags.ejs	Tags	<%= __('index.tagcloud.title') %>
post.ejs	Home	<%= __('page.home') %>
post.ejs, index.ejs	by	<%= __('page.authoredby') %>
index.ejs	<%= theme.excerpt_link %>	<%= __('index.navlinks.continue') %>

5. Save the files – next, fire up a Node.js terminal session.

6. Change the working folder to the myblog folder, and at the prompt enter hexo clean && hexo generate && hexo server -no-optional, and then press Enter.

7. Once done, refresh your browser window (or browse to http://localhost:4000 if it is not running). If all is well, we should not see any immediate change.

8. Go ahead and change the title value on line 4 from Coffee to Apple in the en. yml file that we had open in the previous exercise – save the file, refresh the browser, and this should update. If all is well, we should see the change appear, as indicated in this example (Figure 9-3) – don't forget to change the value back!

Figure 9-3. *The results of updating the en.yml file*

At this stage, we've updated our theme files – we should be good to go, right? Well, yes...and not quite. There are still some more changes we need to make around how we switch languages, but for now, let's take a look at the changes we've made, to see how they work in more detail.

Understanding what happened

Although we've made a series of changes to update our theme in the last exercise, in reality, there is one step that stands above the rest: step 3. It's this step that enables support in our theme for different languages. Sure, we have to specify which, but without the use of __(...) in our theme, it doesn't matter which language we select, as Hexo will use the English version instead!

We kicked off this exercise by making sure that we set the `language:` value to en for English; we then modified the opening `<html>` tag to reference en as a language value for English. Next up, we then used the __() function to switch out hard-coded text and replace it with references to the appropriate label from the YAML language files. We then completed the exercise by regenerating our content so that we could display the updated pages in our browser.

Right, it's crunch time: time to test our updated blog! But...we've just tested it, surely? Well, yes, we have, but only for English. What about French? There is an excellent reason for this, and it's not just to do with making sure our changes work! There are broader implications around how we structure our content, but for now, let's see what happens if we update our blog to display French instead of English.

Testing the changes

So far, we've updated the labels for our blog to reference entries in a YAML data file. We've tested it with English, and this isn't showing any *visual* change – which is a good thing!

The real magic comes when we update our _config.yml file to show French support; what would you expect to see if we did that now? Let's find out.

SWITCHING TO FRENCH SUPPORT

To see what happens, make sure you stop your blog, and then run through these steps:

1. First, we need to make a change in the _config.yml file – for this, crack the file open in a text editor and scroll down to the language: entry.

2. Change the en to fr – this is the code Hexo uses to enable French support. Save and close the file; then fire up a Node.js terminal session, or switch to one if you already have it open.

3. At the prompt, make sure you are in the myblog folder as the working directory; then enter these commands in turn, pressing Enter after each:

   ```
   hexo new post "Test de prise en charge de la langue FR" --lang fr
   hexo new post "Testing FR Language support" --lang en
   ```

4. Next, enter the usual regeneration command at the prompt:

   ```
   hexo clean && hexo generate && hexo server -no-optional
   ```

5. Switch to your browser – if all is well, you should see the posts listed in your index page, as indicated in Figure 9-4.

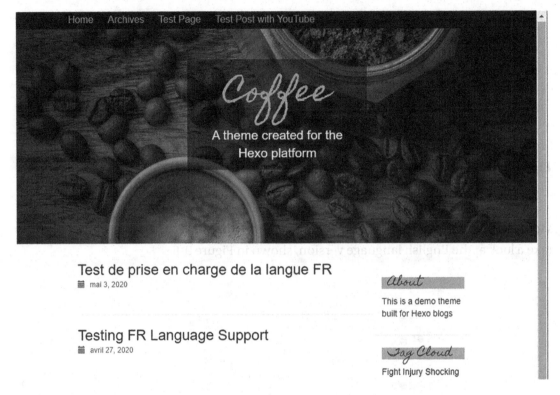

Figure 9-4. *Testing French language support*

Hold on a moment – something doesn't look right, does it? We've created a French-language post, yet our label content is still in English – at least in the sidebar! What gives…?

Understanding the impact of our changes

Don't fret – we've created a French-language post or at least the title for one. The issue here is that we still have at least one more alteration to make; before we do so, let me explain what is going on and why our demo isn't showing the results we expected to see.

To prove that we have indeed written (the stub for) a French-language post, click the link for the "Test de prise en charge de la langue FR." You will see that it is showing the post, but not only that, it is also showing labels in French – including the title. I'll bet you're confused now…!

The trick here lies in *how we created our post.* Hexo accepts the --lang parameter, into which we specified both en and fr in separate commands. It has the effect of introducing the lang attribute in the markup file for this post, as shown in Figure 9-5.

```
---
title: Test de prise en charge de la langue FR
lang: fr
date: 2020-05-03 08:54:24
tags:
---
```

Figure 9-5. *Verifying language support in the FR post*

Try opening the markdown file for "Test de prise en charge de la langue FR" in the \source_posts folder of the myblog project folder – you will see the tag present. Let's take a look at the English language version, shown in Figure 9-6.

```
---
title: Testing Language Support
lang: en
date: 2020-04-27 20:47:25
tags:
---
```

Figure 9-6. *...and that the EN post has a similar property set*

In the first screenshot, we've specified fr for French – hence why we saw the page displayed in French when clicking the link for this post. As the second one set en for English, the post and page titles reverted to English when switching back to the main index page.

It means that (at least in the case of our demo) we can override languages on a per-post basis. While we set fr in the _config.yml file, we can override this by specifying a different language for the lang attribute within the post.

Making support more consistent

This use of two different language values can get confusing...!

To make matters worse, Hexo also accepts a lang parameter in both the permalink: and new_post_name properties that both sit within the _config.yml file – it would look something like this:

```
permalink: :lang/category/:title/
new_post_name: :lang/:title.md
```

However, I would counsel against using this format, for two good reasons:

- We can create the posts, but it is near impossible to create a suitable index file within the subfolders for each language.

- We can't filter out any posts, not in a targeted language from within the `index.ejs` file (used to create the main summary index).

It means that our blog will need to have content in a single language – this works better from an SEO perspective, and given that content can be automatically deployed, it is no great hardship.

There is, however, one change we can make to our demo to ensure that we are using labels in the right language throughout the site. It involves updating the `<html>` tag we've implemented in the `index.ejs` file. Let's take a look in more detail.

UPDATING LANGUAGE RECOGNITION

To set our blog to correctly identify the language used, stop it, and then make this change:

1. Fire up the layout.ejs file from within `\themes\coffee\layout` folder, and change this property as indicated:

    ```
    <html lang="<%= config.language %>">
    ```

2. Save the file.

3. Next, fire up a Node.js terminal (or switch to one if you have it running already), and then make sure the working folder is `myblog`.

4. At the prompt, run this command:

    ```
    hexo clean && hexo generate && hexo server -no-optional
    ```

5. If all is well, we should see `http://localhost:4000` appear in a browser window – we can't do anything about Hexo showing posts in English and French (when we would want it to not show both), but we at least have all of the labels in French language (Figure 9-7).

203

Figure 9-7. Proof that our blog is displaying French labels

Okay, so some of the content is still in English, but this is just post content – the key point here is that all of the labels and main title should now be in French! This simple change does highlight some important issues, so let's take a breather and explore what this change means for us in terms of language support in our blog.

Breaking apart the code

As exercises go, this last one was probably one of the shortest in the book, but one that has had the biggest impact! Why? Well, the answer to that lies in one line of code. Let me explain what I mean.

We worked through a few steps, but in reality, the first step was the most important:

```
<html lang="<%= config.language %>">
```

Here, we set Hexo to take the value of our targeted language directly from the configuration file. It means that no matter what language code we set there, it will permeate through the site. It removes any ambiguity around which language is used and makes it all the more important that we focus on using one language for each instance of our blog. The final step in that exercise was to run the by now familiar hexo clean and regeneration commands so that we can see the updated content appear on our site.

Let's crack on. There is one more area we should cover, and that is the provision of support for RTL languages. Not every language available worldwide follows the same format; we must make allowances for languages such as Arabic when using Hexo. Fortunately, the changes we need to make are not complicated; let's explore what these are in more detail.

Allowing for RTL languages

Although many languages worldwide follow the same left-to-right format, this is not the case for all: some languages use the reverse, and this is something we need to cater for when creating blogs within Hexo.

The great thing about Hexo is that there is very little additional work required to make this happen; in most cases, we just need to use a CSS attribute such as `direction: rtl` to reverse the content. The trick, though, comes in making sure we apply this to the right elements so that we don't end up with a blog that looks back to front!

Other than this, we can use the same process to create a suitable label file as we've done before – with this in mind, let's take a look at the steps we need to take, along with considering how we style RTL text in our blog.

Adding in Arabic support ·

In the next demo, we're going to add in support for Arabic – it's one of many RTL languages available worldwide, but an excellent example of how a culturally different language can affect things when working in Hexo. At this point, I should point out that this exercise is purely about the **technical** steps required to add in RTL languages – I can't claim any accuracy for the content of each label!

ADDING IN ARABIC SUPPORT

Adding in support for RTL languages only requires a few changes – to make it happen, stop your blog, and then follow these steps:

1. First, we need to create our language file – for this, crack open your text editor, and copy in the following code, saving it as `ar.yml` in the languages folder under your theme folder:

```
index:
  title: هيكسو عملي | الصفحة الرئيسية
  header:
    title: قهوة
    description: موضوع تم إنشاؤه لمنصة Hexo
  menu:
    Home: الصفحة الرئيسية
    Archives: أرشيف
    Test: صفحة الاختبار
    YTPage: Test Post with YouTube
  about:
    title: حول
  tagcloud:
    title: علامة سحابة
  archivelist:
    title: أرشيف
  categories:
    title: التصنيفات
  pagination:
    forward: التالي
    backward: السابق
  navlinks:
    continue: أكمل القراءة...
page:
  home: الصفحة الرئيسية
  authoredby: بواسطة
```

2. Next, we need to alter the _config.yml file, to recognize and use the new language file – open the file, and replace the value against `language:` with ar.

3. If we ran the usual generation commands at this point, we would see the text appear, but it won't look great! To fix that, we need to add the following styling into the styles.css file, in the `themes\coffee`

    `\source\css\` folder. Add this code at the top of the page, before the @font-face declaration:

    ```
    h4 { direction: rtl; padding: 3px; }
    .blog-sidebar { padding-left: 30px; }
    div.sidebar-module, .main { direction: rtl; }
    div.post-thumbnail { float: right; margin-left: 15px;}
    ```

4. Save the file.

5. Next, fire up a Node.js terminal (or switch to one if you have it running already), and then make sure the working folder is myblog.

6. At the prompt, run this command:

    ```
    hexo clean && hexo generate && hexo server -no-optional
    ```

7. If all is well, we should see `http://localhost:4000` appear in a browser window – we can't do anything about the "duplicate" posts, but we at least have all of the labels in the Arabic language (Figure 9-8), shown overleaf.

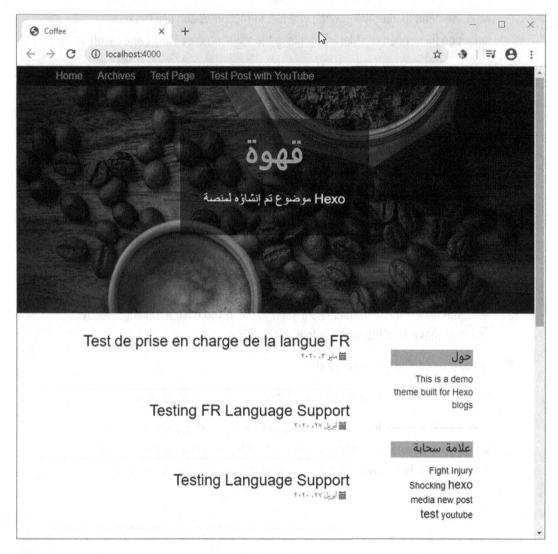

Figure 9-8. Our blog, now in the Arabic language

Perfect – with just a few changes, we've managed to introduce support for RTL languages, such as Arabic or Persian. The changes we've made may only be minor, but they all play an essential role in ensuring content can be displayed correctly. Granted, the text still shows some English, but it's the principle that counts – I'm not an Arabic speaker, so I must leave that to the experts!

Understanding how our code works

Although the changes we've made are only minor, it's essential to consider what we've done. We've already produced a couple of language files to support localizing our blog, so there is nothing new to constructing our Arabic language file. We've used the same structure as before, but this time added in translations using Google Translate.

However, we've had to go one step further: making sure the styling also reflected the nature of these languages. The easy step would have been to simply add `direction: rtl` across the `html` element in our style sheet.

Making this change would work, but only to a certain extent – everything would have been flipped, including the position of our main content and sidebar! It's not something we would want, hence adding `direction: rtl` to only those elements that needed it. Adding this means we can selectively reverse the direction of text and labels while maintaining the same layout as a standard LTR language would use.

Summary

The ability to communicate in a different language is a fundamental part of our modern world – I've always been a great believer in at least trying to communicate with someone in their native tongue and not just assume they speak English.

Although Hexo has a few shortcomings when it comes to incorporating language support, we've touched on several useful tools that will at least allow us to add some essential support – let's recap on what we've covered in this chapter.

We kicked off by exploring the basic principles of how Hexo caters for language support, since it uses YAML files to store labels and a built-in language function to reference content at build time. We then moved onto creating our first language file in English (then in French), before exploring the broader topic of language support in Hexo and how this might affect us when it comes to providing content in different languages.

Next up, we then moved onto adapting our theme to reference labels in the files – we then saw how, despite using them, we still had content appearing in English. We explored the reasons why this might happen and saw how, with a simple change, we could make support more consistent across the blog. We then finished with a look at what needs to happen when adding in languages such as Arabic or Persian, and although the same core process remains, we need to finesse the styling to ensure content is displayed correctly on the page.

Right, it's time to ramp things up! If I were to mention the words "ecommerce" and "architecture," some of you might think, *We need some form of database...*, right? Mmm – what if I said we could produce a Hexo blog that sold products, *without* the need for a database? I can see you thinking that this is not possible – allow me to enlighten you, as we go shopping in the next chapter.

CHAPTER 10

Creating an eCommerce Site

Online shopping is big business, and multiplying year on year – eMarketer reported in mid-2019 that ecommerce would grow by 10.9% to over $140 billion, with almost 60% of this attributable to mobile devices alone! This share is set to increase to a shade over 70% by the year 2023... It is easy to see why physical retail is suffering. After all, who wants to spend time in crowded stores when one can do it from the comfort of their own home? "However, what if I already have a blog and want to move over?" I hear you ask. Moving to Hexo won't be an issue: Hexo supports the migration of content from existing systems such as WordPress, which it achieves through the use of migrator plugins.

But I digress – back to reality. Up until now, we've worked on producing an operational blog, with some added flair in the form of multiple-language support. We can extend this so-called "flair" by adding in another feature – what about buying products from our blog?

Although we usually use blogs to express our opinions, there may be occasions where you might want to sell a limited range of products. It doesn't matter if they are ones you've made or sourced from other companies – we still need a mechanism to allow customers to buy them!

There's no need to create something by hand for this; we can easily make use of a hosted system such as Snipcart to provide simple ecommerce facilities directly from within our site. For this chapter, we'll explore what Snipcart is and learn how to implement it within our site, so it becomes an integral part of what we offer to our customers.

Setting the scene

> *Ladies and gentlemen, I'd like to welcome you to GoCoffee, our online coffee pod store!*

211

© Alex Libby 2020
A. Libby, *Practical Hexo*, https://doi.org/10.1007/978-1-4842-6089-0_10

Our work thus far has focused on a blog created in the myblog folder. For this chapter, we're going to switch tack and create an entirely new blog. There is a good reason for doing this, which will become clearer later in this chapter – for now, let's focus on creating this new blog.

Our new blog will center around a prototype of a mini ecommerce store, called GoCoffee – it will initially sell a limited range of coffee pods, which we can expand on in the future. To give you a flavor of what the finished article will look like, we can see a (partial) screenshot in Figure 10-1.

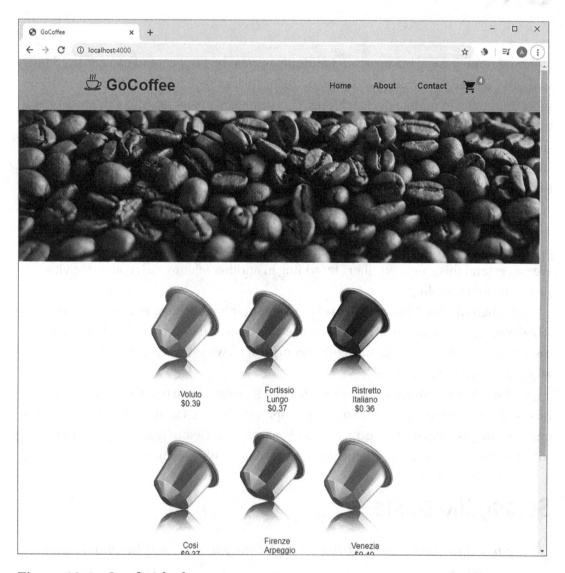

Figure 10-1. *Our finished ecommerce store*

Now, you might be thinking, *I don't see any posts there!* That is indeed true and deliberate: for this project, we're going to take things further than you might expect to see when combining a blog with an online store. Sure, we'll have the typical elements that you would expect to see, such as the shopping basket, product descriptions, and the like. Let's make a start first on building our store, and I will reveal all.

Getting prepared

To get our store off the ground, we need to do some preparatory work – yes, unfortunately, it is a necessary evil, but without it, we won't have our store! There are a few things we need to do, so let's work through the list:

- We first need to register for a Snipcart account, which we can do at `https://snipcart.com/` – this offers free access when used for testing purposes, although it will only provide a limited number of features while testing.

- We will also need a copy of the code download that accompanies this book – we'll use it to get ready copies of some of the media and files used in this project.

- We also need some images. I've sourced them from the Pexels image library at `https://www.pexels.com/`; they are all free to use. For licensing reasons, I've not included them in the code download that accompanies this book, but you can download them from these URLs:

  - `https://www.pexels.com/photo/close-up-photography-of-roasted-coffee-beans-773958/`

  - `https://www.pexels.com/photo/shallow-focus-photography-of-cafe-late-982612/`

  - `https://www.pexels.com/photo/close-up-of-coffee-cup-324028/`

- In addition to the stock images, we also need a shopping basket icon. I've sourced this from `https://www.flaticon.com/free-icon/shopping-cart_60992`; feel free to use something else if you prefer. The icon will be available in the code download that accompanies this book.

- We need some placeholder text for two pages that we will create –
  About Us and Contact. For this, the Lorem Ipsum generator is
  perfect – you can get suitable copy online from the Lorem Ipsum
  generator at `https://lipsum.com/feed/html`.

- We also need some form of color, or our site will look very plain! To
  help here, I've used the color palette generator at `http://colormind.io/image/` to sample the coffee bean image used to produce this
  palette:

  - #928995 – First shade of dark grayish violet

  - #2D2227 – Very dark pink

  - #855446 – Moderately dark red

  - #C3AAA2 – Grayish red

  - #97949E – second shade of dark grayish violet

- There is one last thing that we need, which is a GitHub account – I
  know it might seem a little extreme to have multiple accounts, but
  it makes it much easier to publish! The account needs to be set up
  and configured to viewable using the URL format of `https://XXXXX.github.io` (where XXXXX is your account name).

If you're not sure how to do this, take a look back at Chapter 7 – this details the
process for creating a new account and getting the repository prepared for use.

Okay, we have everything we need in place, so let's crack on and set up our base site,
ready to accept products.

Setting up the base site

As is the case with all projects, we must start somewhere – for us, it will be to set up a
new instance of a Hexo blog, ready for us to customize the look and feel. Throughout this
chapter, we will gradually turn a blog into a fully featured micro-store – or at least as far
as we can within the confines of what is provided by Snipcart!

That aside, there are two things we need to bear in mind while creating our micro-site:

- The instructions will assume you are using Windows, as this is the author's preferred platform for code development; please adjust if you use Linux or macOS as your preferred platform.

- You may notice that we won't be running the hexo generate process until the blog is complete – don't worry, this is intentional! We have a fair few steps to work through, and running this process might end up failing until all of the changes are in place.

Let's crack on and make a start with setting up our blog as part of the first exercise.

CREATING THE INITIAL BLOG

To get our base blog structure in place, work through these steps. We will set up our project in a folder called eshop; please change it accordingly if you prefer to use a different name:

1. We first need to install a new instance of a blog – for this, fire up a Node.js terminal session, and change the working folder to C:.

2. At the prompt, enter this command and press Enter:

    hexo init eshop

3. Once done, change the working folder to be eshop; at the next prompt, run this command to install a new instance of the blog: npm install

4. Once complete, fire up your browser, and navigate to http://localhost:4000 – if all is well, you will see our blog shell appear, using the standard Landscape theme provided by Hexo.

With the blog now in place, we can start to modify it:

5. First, we need to create a theme folder for it – navigate to the eshop folder in your file manager and then into the themes folder, and add a new folder called prague.

6. Inside this folder, create two new folders – one called layout and the other called source. Inside the layout folder, add a new folder called _partial; go ahead and add a css folder inside the source folder.

7. We now need to copy over the prepared styles for this demo – from the code download, go ahead and extract the `styles.css` file and place it inside the `css` folder created in the previous step.

8. With our style sheet in place, we now need to add another `_config.yml` file into the root of the theme folder (i.e., inside `prague`) – this will take care of some theme-specific entries we will be adding later in this chapter.

9. One final change (for now) is to add in an API key needed to interact with Snipcart – for this, log into your Snipcart account at `https://app. snipcart.com/`, and then click Dashboard followed by the head symbol to the top right of the page.

10. Scroll down to API Keys in the menu that appears to the right – you need to add this to the main _config.yml file at the root of the eshop folder, in this format:

```
# SnipCart API key
snipcart_api_key: <your API key>
```

We also need to add in some additional pages or partials – these won't take effect just yet but will be in place ready for when we begin to assemble and process the main index and product pages. With this in mind, crack open your editor, and run through these steps:

1. The first file we need to create takes care of the site title and associated meta tags – this will sit in the `prague\layout\_partial` folder. Go ahead and add the following code to a new file, saving it as `head.ejs` into this folder:

```
<meta charset="utf-8">
<title><%- config.title %></title>
<%- css('/css/styles.css') %>

<!-- Favicon -->
<% if (theme.favicon_url){ %>
  <link rel="icon" href="<%- url_for(theme.favicon_url) %>"
  type="image/x-icon" />
<% } %>

<!-- Meta description tag -->
<% if (config.description){ %>
  <meta name="description" content="<%= config.description %>">
<% } %>
```

2. Next, we need to create a file that looks after the header of our site – this will contain the hero banner and menu. Save this as header.ejs into the same _partial folder from the previous step:

```
<div class="headtitle">
  <img src="../images/coffee.svg">
  <a href="/">
    <h1 class="blog-title"><%= config.title %></h1>
    <p><%= config.description %></p>
  </a>
</div>
<%- partial('_partial/menu') %>
```

3. The next file to create will look after our menu – add this code to a new file, saving it as menu.ejs into the same _partial folder as before:

```
<nav id="menu">
  <ul>
    <% for (var i in theme.menu){ %>
      <li><a class="blog-nav-item" href="<%- url_for(theme.menu[i]) %>">
      <%= i %></a></li>
    <% } %>
    <a href="#" class="snipcart-checkout">
        <img src="../images/shopping-cart.svg" aria-hidden="true">
    </a>
    <span class="snipcart-summary">
      <span class="snipcart-total-items"></span>
    </span>
  </ul>
</nav>
```

4. We have two more files to work on – for this next one, we need to add some menu entries into the _config.yml file. Crack open the one located in the prague folder, and add this at the start of the file:

```
# Header
menu:
  Home: /
  About: /about/
  Contact: /contact/
```

5. The final file we need to add in is `layout.ejs` – for reasons of space, we need to source this one from the code download. Go ahead and extract a copy of this file to the `\prague\layout` folder.

Phew! A fair few steps there! It may look like a real mishmash of files that won't mean anything yet, but that will change once we begin to add in the main index and additional pages. That aside, it's still important to understand what we've done here, so let's take a moment to review the changes we've made in more detail.

Understanding what happened

When beginning a new project, there are inevitably several steps we have to work through to get to a suitable starting point. With Hexo, we can create a blog with very few steps – but to get it to show as a micro-store requires a lot more work.

In this exercise, we started on the process of creating our blog, before beginning to adapt it to display as our store. We built several partial (or template) files and imported the predefined styles from the code download that accompanies this book.

We then moved onto customizing the code – we started with the `head.ejs` file, which took care of adding a title and meta tags to the head of our site. We then created a `header.ejs` file to look after (no surprises) the header, before assembling `menu.ejs` to take care of our menu. For the latter to take effect, we also added the menu entries to the `_config.yml` file.

We then rounded out the exercise by importing a copy of the `layout.ejs` file from the code download – the majority of it is standard HTML markup. It does use a couple of instances of Hexo code, such as `<%- partial('_partial/head') %>` to import the `head.ejs` file into the page and `<% if (config.snipcart_api_key) { %>`, which determines whether we should be importing the source files needed for our Snipcart integration (more on this, later in the book).

There is one entry of interest though – and one which might appear confusing: `<% if (page.current_url == "") { %>`. At first glance, checking to see what URL we are displaying is standard fare, but...checking for an empty URL? The reason we're doing this is that `current_url` checks for the presence of a *relative path* and **not** the base URL defined in the `_config.yml` file. In our case, this is perfect – we only want to see the header image on the main index page. As this doesn't return a relative path, it will only display the image on that page!

Okay, let's crack on. Our blog is in place; time for us to develop the all-important product gallery! The creation will use the `hexo new` process to create a set of posts, to which we will use the predefined style sheet to reformat the content. Let's take a look at what's involved in more detail.

Building the gallery

So far, our bare blog shell is in place, with some of the customizations we need to turn it into a mini ecommerce store. If we were to run the by now familiar Hexo generation process, our blog would look terrible – it's more likely to fail, though, as we still have pages to add in!

For our next exercise, we're going to start correcting that, by adding in the main index page to display products, once we add them in a little later in this chapter. We only need to make two changes, which is to add the main product summary file and a partial to handle the display of each product on the main index. Let's take a look at the code needed to effect this change in more detail.

BUILDING THE GALLERY

To set up the main product gallery, crack open your text editor, and follow these steps:

1. We need to add in two files – the first one will be the main index. For this, add the following code to a new file, saving it as `index.ejs` in the `\prague\layout` folder:

```
<span id="shop">
  <% page.posts.forEach(function(item, index){ %>
    <%- partial('_partial/post-index', {item: item}) %>
  <% }); %>
</span>
```

2. The second file to add in will take care of displaying the summary details of each product on the main index – for this, add the following code to a new file, saving it as `post-index.ejs` in the `\prague\layout\_partial` folder:

```
<div class="grid">
  <div class="post-image">
    <a href="<%- url_for(item.path) %>">
      <img src="<%- url_for(item.image) %>" alt="<%- item.name || "Untitled" %>">
    </a>
  </div>
  <div class="post-details">
    <a href="<%- url_for(item.path) %>"><%- item.name || "Untitled"
    %></a>
    <div class="price">$<%= item.price.toFixed(2) %></div>
  </div>
</div>
```

3. Save both files and close them – you can keep the editor open, as we will use it very shortly in the next exercise.

A nice simple change in comparison to the first exercise, which, I am sure you will agree, was something of a monster! Although the changes won't mean a great deal just yet, that will change once we add in and process the product pages; in the meantime, let's take a look at the code in more detail, as it contains some useful tips when working with Hexo and Snipcart.

Breaking apart the code

Over the years, I've become known for writing monster exercises. In my defense, though, it's not something I can always avoid; it all hangs around what makes sense when completing the activities! I do try to follow them with something much shorter – this last exercise certainly being a case in point.

We kicked off by creating the initial `index.ejs` file – this we used to position all of the products onto the summary page in a grid format. Much of what we've used is standard markup, but this block is of particular note:

```
<% page.posts.forEach(function(item, index){ %>
  <%- partial('_partial/post-index', {item: item}) %>
<% }); %>
```

Here we've used the page object to reference all posts; we iterated through each markdown file using forEach and combined content from them with the post-index partial to create each product page. We passed through item as an object reference, so that we can apply the various properties such as name and price to the page.

Moving on, we then built the post-index partial; in this one, we used three functions of particular note:

- url_for() – This takes care of working out where the image URL passed in as a parameter is located and combines it with the base URL (or url in _config.yml) to form a properly constructed URL.

- item – This is a reference to each (markdown) page so that we can pick off each element such as item.name or item.price and position them on the processed page.

- The standard JavaScript method, .toFixed() – we use this to display all of the prices to two decimal places; without it, we might otherwise end up with values such as $0.4, which won't look right.

Excellent! We now have a working product gallery, or at least we will do once we come to process all of the pages! Rest assured we will do this, but before we do, we still have a handful of pages to add to our demo. I'm talking about the About Us and Contact pages, along with the individual product pages; let's take a look first at the product pages and how we get these set up in our micro-site.

Creating the product page and content

We're making steady but good progress toward creating our mini online store. The blog shell is in place, we have our main product gallery built, and the main index will look presentable once we get to processing the code into static HTML later in this chapter.

For now, though, we have a small number of changes to make before we can turn our attention to enabling Snipcart – the first of these is to set up the individual product pages and add suitable content to them. Let's take a look at what is involved in more detail.

DEMO: CREATING THE PRODUCT PAGE AND CONTENT

To get our product page up and running, follow these steps:

1. The first task is to create our product pages – for this, we need to fire up a Node.js terminal session, and then change the working folder to that of the eshop folder.

2. At the prompt enter this command and press Enter:

   ```
   hexo new post "Cosi"
   ```

3. Repeat this a further five times, but this time, substitute `Cosi` for each of these words in turn: `Firenze-Arpeggio`, `Fortissio-Lungo`, `Ristretto-Italiano`, `Venezia`, and `Voluto`.

4. This step will result in six markdown files in the _posts folder – we now need to add in the content for each page. In the code download, there are six files with the appropriate markup for each of the posts. Copy the contents of each into the relevant file – for example, the contents of `Voluto.txt` into `Voluto.md` and so on. Save the files and close them.

5. Next, we need to create our post (or product) template – for this, crack open your text editor and add the following code to a new file, saving it as `post.ejs`. We'll go through it block by block, starting with adding the container <div> element:

   ```
   <div class="grid">
   ...
   </div>
   ```

6. Next, we need to add in the elements that will hold the content – first up is a `<div>` to contain a full-sized version of the product image. Add this in between the `<div>...</div>` statements from the previous step:

   ```
   <div class="post-image">
       <img src="<%- url_for(page.image) %>" alt="<%- page.name %>">
   </div>
   ```

7. Next, we need to add in the product details – this comes in two parts, the first of which displays the product name, price, and description:

```
<div class="post-details">
  <div class="price"><h3><%- page.name %></h3></div>
  <div class="price">$<%- page.price.toFixed(2) %></div>
  <div class="price"><%- page.content %></div>
```

8. The second part is the call that passes details to Snipcart – add this in for now, but we will go through this in more detail later in this chapter:

```
  <% if (page.product) { %>
    <!-- Enter Snipcart buy button here -->
    <button class="snipcart-add-item"
      data-item-id="<%- page.product.id %>"
      data-item-price="<%- page.price %>"
      data-item-description="<%- page.content %>"
      data-item-image="../<%- page.image %>"
      data-item-name="<%- page.name%>"
      data-item-url="<%- page.permalink %>">
      Add to cart
    </button>
  <% } %>
</div>
```

9. Save the file and close it – keep the editor and Node.js terminal sessions open though, as we will use both to add in the remaining pages in the next exercise.

I'm sure you will agree that this was a much easier exercise than the previous one. *Chuckle!* Most of it uses a technique we've used before when we created the original blog earlier in the book – however, the code in post.ejs uses a fundamental approach that is worth exploring in more detail, so let's take a closer look.

Exploring the code in detail

So, what did we do in this last exercise? Well, it centered around two tasks: creating the pages using the standard hexo new command and creating the post template to display our product details.

We kicked off by using the now familiar `hexo new post` command to create six pages – one each for the six coffee pods we will be selling in our mock ecommerce site. We then copied in the markdown content from text files from the code download – this resulted in six markdown files, looking similar to the Voluto one shown in Figure 10-2, shown overleaf.

Things get more interesting, though, once we turn our attention to the `post.ejs` file – here, we added in the various elements that we will use to position product details on the page and display the Snipcart add to cart button. The first element we added in was the image; we then followed this with the product name, price, and description.

```
name: Voluto
image: images/yellow.png
price: 0.39
product:
  id: 1
---
A blend of pure and lightly roas
reveals sweet and biscuity flavo
fruity note.
```

Figure 10-2. *An extract from one of the markdown files*

The slightly more substantial block that followed was for the Snipcart add to cart button; as we're not using databases, all of the details have to be passed manually from the product page, at the point of adding items to the basket. We'll touch more on this a little later in this chapter, as using Snipcart opens up some exciting possibilities for us to follow up in the future.

Okay, let's move on. We now have product pages in place; we have two more pages to create before our site is "page complete." For the next exercise, we're going to create placeholder pages for About Us and Contact; we won't add in the functionality that we might otherwise expect but put something to simulate the presence of these pages in our site. Let's take a look at what's involved – you should by now be relatively familiar with at least part of what is coming in this exercise!

Adding supplementary pages

We're almost at the crux of our demo, which is to add in a shopping cart feature – before we do so, we need to complete one more step, which is to add in some simulated page content.

This next task will be just the About Us and Contact pages for now, but as we will see, we can easily use the same option to add in more pages at a later date. We will use the same process we've seen from earlier demos, so without further ado, let's dive in and get the pages set up ready for use.

DEMO: CREATING THE ABOUT US AND CONTACT PAGES

The two pages we will create are "About Us" and "Contact" – these won't be fully operational in the same way as standard ecommerce sites, but act as placeholders to simulate what we might expect to see on a typical online retail outlet. To get these pages in place, follow these steps:

1. We now need to create two additional pages – one for an "About Us" and another for "Contact." To do this, fire up a Node.js terminal session, and then change the working folder to that of the eshop folder.

2. At the prompt enter this command and press Enter:

    ```
    hexo new page "About"
    ```

3. Repeat step 2, but replace the word "About" with "Contact":

    ```
    Hexo new page "Contact"
    ```

4. We're also going to add in a sitemap as an extra – for this step, we will use the hexo-generator-sitemap plugin, available from `https://github.com/hexojs/hexo-generator-sitemap`. At the prompt, enter this command and press Enter:

    ```
    npm install hexo-generator-sitemap --save-dev
    ```

5. Next, revert to your text editor, and open the _config.yml file from within the \ themes\prague folder, and then add this code in at the bottom:

```
sitemap:
    path: sitemap.xml
    template: ./sitemap_template.xml
    rel: false
```

6. Save the file and close it.

7. Although we have placeholder pages in place, we need something to display content from the markdown files – for this, revert to your text editor, and then add the following to a new file, saving it as page.ejs in the \themes\ prague\layout folder:

```
<div class="pagecontent">
  <h3><%- page.title %></h3>
  <img src="<%- page.image%>">
  <p><%- page.content %></p>
</div>
```

8. We can now finally run the Hexo generation process! At the prompt, enter this command and press Enter:

```
hexo clean && hexo generate && hexo server -no-optional
```

9. If all is well, we should see something akin to the screenshot shown in Figure 10-3.

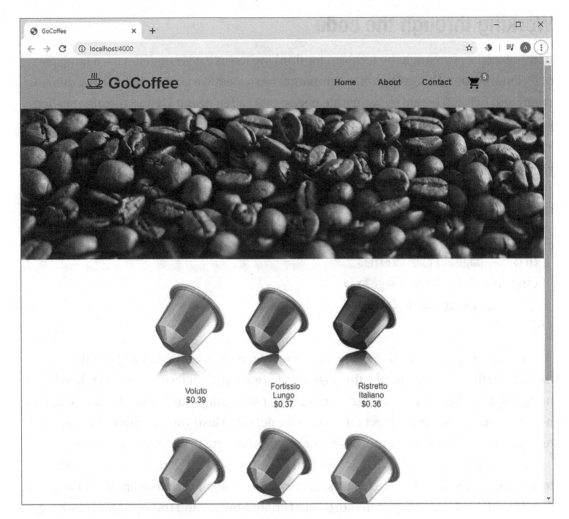

Figure 10-3. *Our (almost) completed mini store*

For the most part, this exercise used a technique we've already worked with from earlier demos, inasmuch as we used the hexo new command to create pages for our placeholder content. However, we've added in some Hexo code to form our page template – let's take a moment to review this in more detail.

Working through the code

In this exercise, you might be forgiven for thinking it was a case of déjà-vu – a large part of it centers around a now familiar command, hexo new! We kicked off by using this command twice to create two separate pages, one called About Us and the other called Contact. This step resulted in creating two folders in each case, stored at the root of the source folder – each folder contains an index.md file that holds the markdown content for each page.

Where things get interesting is in the post.ejs file we then created – here it is as a reminder:

```
<div class="pagecontent">
  <h3><%- page.title %></h3>
  <img src="<%- page.image%>">
  <p><%- page.content %></p>
</div>
```

In this code, we've used the page object to reference specific tags within the markdown file. So, for example, the page title for each product would be referenced using page.title, the page image coming from page.image, and so on. It's important to note that this is a generic object reference – by default, Hexo will use this to format each template of page type when processing the content during the generation process.

Okay, let's crack on. We've now reached the all-important part of this demo, which is to add a shopping cart feature to our site! We've touched on various elements briefly, but this time around, we will go into more detail about how we add this option to our blog.

Adding Snipcart

Okay, I have something of a confession to make: as it so happens, we've already built all of the elements needed to implement Snipcart into our site without realizing it!

There is a good reason for this, though – most of the work required centers around the product pages, which uses the same hexo new post technique from earlier in this book. All we had to do was add in some extra tags to the front matter, to turn them into product pages!

We've added several templates too; most of these, though, are just standard markup files, with only a tiny amount of JavaScript required to interface with Snipcart. Adding the changes to each product page separately wouldn't make sense – it won't give the whole picture as to what needs to happen to implement Snipcart.

With this in mind, we're not going to run through this as a standard demo. Instead, I will walk you through the changes I made to get Snipcart installed; you'll see how they all come together as part of the Snipcart integration.

DEMO WALK-THROUGH: ADDING SNIPCART

Let's take a look at the steps we went through to add Snipcart to our micro-site:

1. The first change we made was to the config.yml file – this was to add in our API key. We got this by logging into our Snipcart account at `https://app.snipcart.com/` and then by clicking Dashboard and the head symbol to the top right of the page. Scrolling down to and clicking the API Keys entry in the menu that appears to the right displays the API key.

2. The next change we made was in the `menu.ejs` file – here, we added in this code, to set up a link to our Snipcart basket:

```
<a href="#" class="snipcart-checkout">
  <img src="../images/shopping-cart.svg" aria-hidden="true">
</a>
```

3. In the same file, we also added in this code – this serves to show the total number of items in our basket:

```
<span class="snipcart-summary">
  <span class="snipcart-total-items"></span>
</span>
```

4. The next change we made was in `layout.ejs` – in this case, we added two entries: one as a `<div>` to store the API key which we call directly from the `_config.yml` file and the other are the links to the various script files used by Snipcart to host our basket facility.

5. This next change does not directly talk to Snipcart but instead uses values from the front matter (or head) of each post markdown file to display details about each product. In this instance, we use `item` as a generic reference to each product (or post) and show the name, image, and price – we display all of these on the main index page as our product gallery.

6. We do something similar in `post.ejs`, where we display the same details, but this time add in a block that provides details to Snipcart for the chosen product.

7. It's important to note that using the `data-` attributes means we can apply values to the button, but as these are not HTML tags, we're not adding unnecessary tags into our code. At the point of clicking the button, we pass these values to Snipcart – Snipcart was written using Vue.js, so handles form submission differently to standard HTML forms.

8. The last stage was to create the six product pages – for this, we used the by now familiar hexo new post process. We then added in the relevant markdown values, using the product: tag as a means to identify those posts to be displayed on the front page as our product gallery.

At this stage, we now have a fully working site – it's time to get it online! Fortunately for us, we can use precisely the same process that we used back in Chapter 7; the only changes are those required to keep this a separate project. Let's revisit and work through these steps so that we can get our site online and available for people to see via the Internet.

Publishing to GitLab

We've completed the build process – the final step is publication! This next step might sound a little scary, but in reality, it should be a little easier now, given as we've already run through the steps back in Chapter 7.

The process is precisely the same for our shop, except for the change of username – this time, though, we're not using any custom plugins that aren't available from NPM, so the upload and build process will be much easier.

To avoid repetition, I've created a copy of the steps we used back in Chapter 7 as a PDF – you can find it in the code download as `Uploading to GitHub.pdf`.

Assuming all works OK, then we will end up with a new site hosted on GitHub Pages, which will look like the screenshot shown in Figure 10-4, shown overleaf.

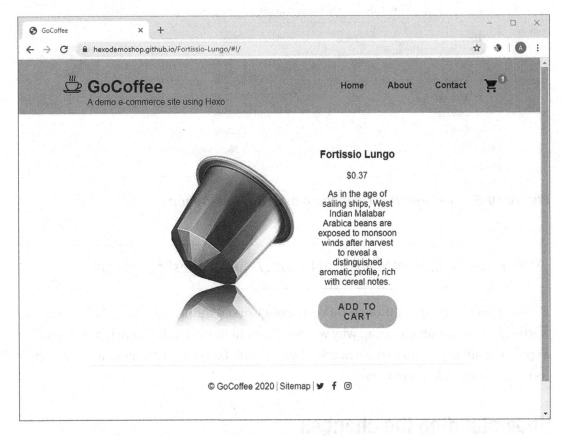

Figure 10-4. *Our completed site hosted on GitHub Pages*

If we take a look at the cloned version after the build, we should end up with something akin to that listed in Figure 10-5.

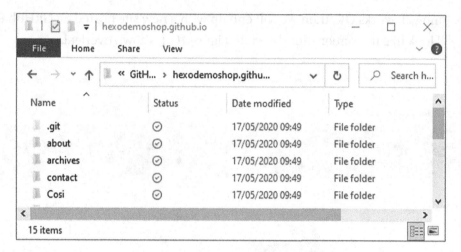

Figure 10-5. *The (updated) cloned area for our demo shop*

You can see the completed article at `https://hexodemoshop.gitlab.io`.

Okay, let's move on. Although we've already worked through the steps before, it's still worth taking a moment to recap why we took them in more detail. There is also a small step that could trip us up that we need to be aware of. Let's take a moment to review the code and changes in more detail.

Understanding the changes

To deploy content on GitHub Pages might seem like a very lengthy task – there are indeed a lot of steps to cover. However, most of them will be a one-off, at least for each repository we set up; updating content will seem like a walk in the park in comparison!

In this instance, we began by setting up a repository using the name `XXXXXX.github.io` (where XXXXX was the username we chose to use). Selecting an appropriate username means we can view the final results online as `https://XXXXX.github.io`. It gives us the combination of a secure website and allows easy updates by others should they find a bug or want to add a feature.

We then used standard Git processes, via GitHub Desktop, to first clone the contents of the repository to our local PCs, before uploading content and publishing it online. At the same time, we configured Travis CI to both build and test our site; this gives an added confidence that our site is working as expected once it has completed. At this point, and assuming it is showing a green tick to confirm a successful build, we can view the site in all its glory via our browser.

If only things were quite that easy ... There is a little sting in this tail, though! During the build process, I received this alert in an email:

The page build completed successfully, but returned the following warning for the `master` branch:

You are attempting to use a Jekyll theme, "prague", which is not supported by GitHub Pages. Please visit https://pages.github.com/themes/ for a list of supported themes.

In reality, it's not as bad as it might sound – the warning is coming from our use of theme: in the _config.yml file. GitHub Pages treats our build process as if we're building Jekyll pages; it only supports a limited subset of themes that have to be installed using Ruby gems. We're not using Ruby gems here, though – as it so happens, the warning only comes during the build process, and as this is indeed a demo site, it's not too critical!

If you want to get rid of the warning, then try changing theme: in the main _config.yml file to remote_theme: to see if this works. I've not done it here, as the warning only comes during the build, so isn't something that should concern us.

Leaving that aside, let's carry on. Now that we have a working site, there are a couple of areas we should explore as a way to wrap up this demo. We've already hinted at one, which is the reason for using a separate blog; the other is to explore what we could potentially do to expand and develop our blog in the future. Let's take a look at the question of architecture first.

Comparing architecture

Throughout this chapter, we've built a separate blog as a mini ecommerce site. However, some of you may be wondering why we decided to go down the route of a separate entity and not just develop the existing project further.

This point is something we should explore in more detail, as it will help frame how you use Hexo. Your primary concern will, of course, be your original requirements (am I blogging, selling, etc.?), but that some of the limitations around using Hexo may determine which approach you can take when using the tool. Let's take a look at some of the points to consider when adding ecommerce using a tool such as Snipcart:

- Creating a new entity opens up an option for those people who don't want to sell lots of different products, but still need the means to offer them for retail. It also allows us to focus on the steps we need to take to create a complete ecommerce entity (granted, complete is perhaps a misnomer here, but you get the idea!).

- Although what we've produced looks nothing like our original blog, we created most of it using steps taken on the existing one – each product "page" (as such) is just a post that we created with the hexo new post command. It means that we could easily add in a blog post around the product being sold – we might need to add in a variable to shift the description from the main part into the header, but this isn't difficult.

- There is one downside though – Hexo doesn't really support a "sub-index" that allows us to display posts from a certain category of the main page; for us, it's a case of all posts will be displayed on the main page, assuming that we don't use a filter mechanism (as we did in our product gallery). This does mean that your product posts may get lost in a sea of posts – it will place greater emphasis on creating top-notch content that encourages good traffic, so that people see the products you have on offer.

- For this particular project, I wanted to push the boundaries of what was possible – admittedly this wasn't as much as I would have liked, given that Snipcart doesn't offer a full feature set in testing mode. However, I think we've created something that is useable and could be developed further with not too much effort; it hopefully shows how ecommerce facilities can be incorporated, without the use of a database that we know will be a security risk!

Hopefully this gives you a few points to consider – Hexo is a great tool, and given its dependence on Node.js, it means we have access to a wide ecosystem of plugins that can help produce a great site that can be used by anyone who visits your blog or ecommerce site.

Taking things further: Where next?

Now that we've completed the project, where can we go, and how can we develop our project further?

Well, Snipcart offers a host of different features we can try out – some are unfortunately not available while we are in test mode, but should you decide to use Snipcart in a production environment, then here are a few ideas to get you started:

- We've created a static list of six products for sale, but what if your needs lie more in adding in random products as part of a blog post? This should absolutely be possible – we already have this code in the `layout.ejs` file, ready for use (albeit commented out at present):

  ```
  <!-- <%- partial('_partial/article-tags', {item: page}) %> -->
  <!-- <%- partial('_partial/article-categories', {item: page}) %> -->
  ```

  We could use this and add tags to each product – this would create the equivalent of a tag cloud that will only display products tagged with an appropriate category. It's a little bit of a poor man's filtering system, but as long as we style it correctly, it could produce something that works! Oh, and we've already covered all of the code required to get this working too...

- One area we could explore is the use of Google Analytics, as well as the whole subject of SEO. Even though we're only offering a small range of products, it's important to make sure that we can track customers, as well as fine-tune the blog and product pages to be as performant as possible from an SEO perspective.

- A simple change we could effect is a default "no photo available" image – we could put an entry into the theme's `_config.yml` file and adapt the `item.image` entries to use the default image if a proper image isn't available.

- Snipcart does have a range of different features that are available that are worth investigating further – two examples that come to mind are offering other currencies and discounts!

- And finally, have you noticed how we don't have a prominent call to action to check out from our blog? Granted, it won't work in quite the same way as a standard ecommerce site, but it would be handy to have a more obvious route to progress to the basket and start the checkout process.

These ideas are just some that we could investigate, to help develop our blog into a more rounded ecommerce offering. At the same time, we should also take a look at the plugin list from the main Hexo site, just in case any plugins could help improve the experience for our customers!

Summary

Although Hexo is primarily a blogging tool, it's simple markdown, and Node.js architecture means we can potentially put it to other uses – including some which you might not immediately consider when using markdown files! Throughout this chapter, we've seen how we could use Hexo to create a simple ecommerce site. Let's take a moment to review what we have learned in this chapter.

We kicked off by setting the scene – understanding that ecommerce has become big business and that a small part of this will come from those who offer products via their blog. We covered the background to creating our project, before setting up the base shell of our blog and beginning to customize it into a mini online store.

Next up, we then concentrated on creating the product gallery and pages before switching our attention to adding in some additional pages to give the site a more rounded feel. We then worked through the steps used to add in Snipcart; we saw how this had been added while creating the various templates, so explored the changes we made to effect our installation.

We then rounded out the chapter by exploring the upload and deployment processes to GitHub Pages – we saw that they are largely identical to the method used back in Chapter 7, with only minor changes to allow for our new project. At the same time, we discussed some of the finer points of why we created a new blog rather than expand on the original, before taking a quick look at some ideas to help finesse and develop the experience for our customers.

And relax... Not for too long, though. We still have one more topic left to cover! Hands up if you've used WordPress before. I'll bet there will be a few of you, right? Well, I've talked about how databases can be a weak point in our site's security, so it's time to do something about it – what if we were to switch from using WordPress to Hexo? Stay with me, and I will reveal how in the next chapter.

CHAPTER 11

Migrating to Hexo

Throughout this book, we've concentrated on creating content from scratch – this is perfect for those of you who don't have an existing blog or might have had one some time ago and it's so out of date there is nothing worth reusing.

A number of these are available for existing platforms; for this chapter, we'll explore what is available and work through how to migrate content over, using WordPress as the basis for our example platform.

Understanding the migration process

One of the great features of Hexo is the ability to import content from multiple blogging platforms; thanks to its plugin architecture, Hexo has plugins available for most of the well-known platforms, such as WordPress, Jekyll, and even RSS feeds!

The trouble is while the *technical* process of exporting content to Hexo is very straightforward, it's what happens afterward that makes matters more complicated. To see what I mean, here are the high-level steps we will have to work through, as part of this migration process:

1. Where possible, assess what plugins we have and remove any that are not essential to your blog.

2. Copy your images and media to a new location, so that we can relink them later.

3. Export posts and pages from your blog into XML files, or take a copy of the markdown files (if your blog already uses them).

© Alex Libby 2020
A. Libby, *Practical Hexo*, https://doi.org/10.1007/978-1-4842-6089-0_11

4.   Use the hexo-migrator-XXXX plugin to import the content –
     where XXXXX is the source platform, such as WordPress or
     RSS. Alternatively, copy the markdown files over, for those blogs
     which don't need a plugin.

5.   Review all content to see what is missing.

6.   Rework images and media content to point to the new location.

7.   Shut down your old blog after some time, once redirected traffic is
     sufficiently low to allow shutdown.

Granted, this is a very high-level process, but as we can already see, the steps
running up to and after the export and import (steps 3 and 4) make this a more
complicated process!

For this chapter, we'll focus primarily on steps 3 and 4, but that aside, it's essential
to fully consider what content you have and whether you can take any steps to reduce
complexity. Are there any plugins that could be retired, for example? What about old
posts – are there any that we can archive? Are you using any user management that could
be affected by the migration? These questions are just some of the ones we have to ask
ourselves, but assuming that you've considered these, let's take a look in more detail as
to how we perform the migration of our content.

Options available for migrating content

For this chapter, we will use WordPress as our example platform – I've chosen it as it's
one I've used before, although the export/import process is similar for most blogging
platforms/tools. The plugin we will use to migrate content is `https://github.com/`
`hexojs/hexo-migrator-wordpress` – this we will install using the same method for most
Hexo-based plugins.

The `hexo-migrator-wordpress` plugin isn't the only migration plugin available;
Hexo supports migration from several blogging tools. It's very likely going to be a plugin
that suits your needs and works similarly to the one we will use in this chapter. A list of
known plugins for migrating content is displayed in Table 11-1.

Table 11-1. *A list of migrator plugins available*

Tool	Plugin name and URL
WordPress	hexo-migrator-wordpress – available from `https://github.com/hexojs/hexo-migrator-wordpress.`
RSS	hexo-migrator-rss – available from `https://github.com/hexojs/hexo-migrator-rss.`
Jekyll	This one doesn't need a plugin – simply move or copy all files in the Jekyll _posts folder to the source/_posts folder in Hexo.
Octopress	This one doesn't need a plugin – simply move (or copy) all files in the Octopress source/_posts folder to the source/_posts folder in Hexo.
Joomla	hexo-migrator-joomla – available from `https://github.com/welksonramos/hexo-migrator-joomla.`

All of these plugins use the same core process, which is `hexo migrate <name of platform> <source of file>` – this makes it very easy to perform the initial migration process. I say initial, as it's not a simple as a lift and shift; as we will find out shortly, there will be some work do afterward!

Before we get stuck into the migration process, though, there is a little housekeeping we need to do. I know it's not my favored task, but it's necessary so that we can complete the migration as smoothly as possible. There's only a handful of items to do, so without further ado, let's cover these off before continuing with the migration process.

Housekeeping

Yes, there are indeed occasions where a little preparation is essential! Throughout this chapter, we will be using WordPress as our example platform; to get the best from the exercises, you will need to avail yourselves with the following tools:

- A working installation of WordPress that has the content you can use to practice migration; I'm using a self-hosted version available locally, although this should also work with versions hosted by third-party providers or via WordPress.com. I will assume you are using WordPress 5.x, which is the latest at the time of writing; please adapt if you are using an older version.

- If you want to host WordPress locally (ideal, as you can practice as much as you like, without any issues), then you will need a local web server – I'm using XAMPP Portable, which is free and requires no prior configuration. It's cross-platform, and versions are available for download from `https://xampp.site/xampp-portable/`.

- If you need to install WordPress from scratch, then I would recommend following the instructions at `https://wordpress.org/support/article/how-to-install-wordpress/`. Do note though that the passwords they use are not suitable for a production environment; as we're working in a development capacity only, this isn't an issue.

- Alternatively, you can try requesting a temporary WordPress install from the Open Source CMS site at `https://www.opensourcecms.com/wordpress/` – it's not something I've tested, so I don't know how well it works, but it might be worth a look.

Okay, with everything hopefully now in place, let's make a start – the first task is to prepare the recipient blog to receive our imported content.

Setting up our new blog

The first task in the migration process is to set up somewhere to receive the exported content – we'll do this as a new blog so that we can practice the migration in complete safety. To do this, we will use the by now familiar `hexo init` command, so it should not take us very long to complete.

For this demo, I will assume that you are working from the root of C: – please adapt the instructions accordingly if you want to change the location.

SETTING UP A NEW BLOG

Let's make a start with setting up a new blog, to receive our exported text:

1. First, fire up a Node.js terminal and change the working folder to the root of your drive.

2. Next, enter this command at the prompt, and press Enter:

   ```
   hexo init migrate
   ```

3. You should see Hexo download and install a new blog, as indicated in Figure 11-1.

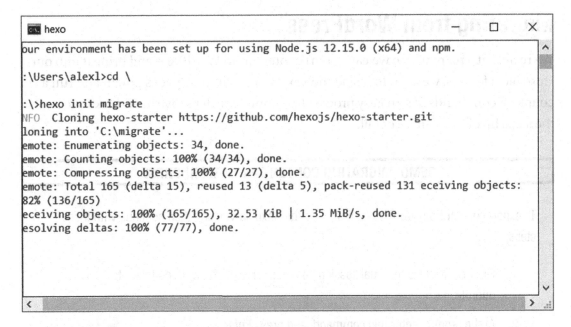

Figure 11-1. *Hexo downloading and installing the new blog instance*

4. Once complete, change the working folder to migrate, and then run this command:

   ```
   hexo clean && hexo generate && hexo server -no-optional
   ```

As we've only just created this blog, you can run hexo server on its own, as we've not yet changed any of the markdown files. Running the preceding command ensures you have a clean build each time.

At this point, we now have a new blog into which we can import our content from WordPress. I would recommend browsing to the `\migrate\source\_posts` folder and removing the contents; it isn't obligatory, but means that the test "Hello World" post won't get lost in a sea of imported posts from WordPress!

Okay, let's move on. Now that we have our recipient blog in place, it's time to begin the migration process. The next step is to export content from WordPress; this will give us an XML file with the content within, although there are some limitations as to what we can export. To find out more, let's dive in and take a look at what this means for us in practice.

Migrating from WordPress

We're now at a point where we can export content from WordPress and bring it into our Hexo blog; for this, we need to install the `hexo-migrator-wordpress` plugin and run a couple of commands. It's an easy process to complete, so let's dive in and take a look at the steps involved in more detail.

DEMO: MIGRATING CONTENT FROM WORDPRESS

To export content from WordPress, first, stop the Hexo server, and then continue with these steps:

1. Fire up a Node.js terminal session, and then change the working folder to migrate.

2. At the prompt, enter this command, and press Enter:

   `npm install hexo-migrator-wordpress –save`

3. Once done, minimize the terminal session for now, as we will need it shortly.

4. Next, switch to your WordPress installation, and then click Tools ➤ Export, as indicated in Figure 11-2.

Figure 11-2. *Triggering the export process in WordPress*

5. On the next screen, click All content, as shown in Figure 11-3.

Figure 11-3. *Options available in WordPress' export function*

6. Selecting this option triggers the export process, which downloads an XML file with this name: `wordpressmigration.WordPress.YYYY-MM-DD.xml`, where YYYY-MM-DD is the date of exporting the content, as shown in Figure 11-4.

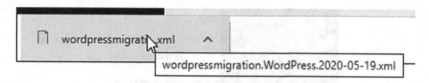

Figure 11-4. *The exported content after downloading*

7. Once completed, revert to your terminal session, and then change the working folder to migrate.

8. At the prompt, enter this command, replacing `wordpressmigration.WordPress.YYYY-MM-DD.xml` with the date shown in the downloaded file name, and then press Enter:

```
hexo migrate wordpress c:\migrate\wordpressmigration
.WordPress.YYYY-MM-DD.xml
```

You can see an example of this in Figure 11-5.

```
Node.js command prompt                                               —   □   ×

C:\migrate>hexo migrate wordpress c:\migrate\wordpressmigration.WordPress.2020-05-19.xml
INFO  Analyzing c:\migrate\wordpressmigration.WordPress.2020-05-19.xml...
INFO  Post found: Hello world!
INFO  Page found: Sample Page
INFO  Page found: Privacy Policy
INFO  3 posts migrated.

C:\migrate>
```

Figure 11-5. *Running the hexo migrate command*

9. Assuming you don't get any errors, then restart the Hexo server by running this command:

```
hexo clean && hexo generate && hexo server -no-optional
```

10. Go ahead and browse to `http://localhost:4000` – if all is OK, you should see your imported WordPress post (Figure 11-6, shown overleaf).

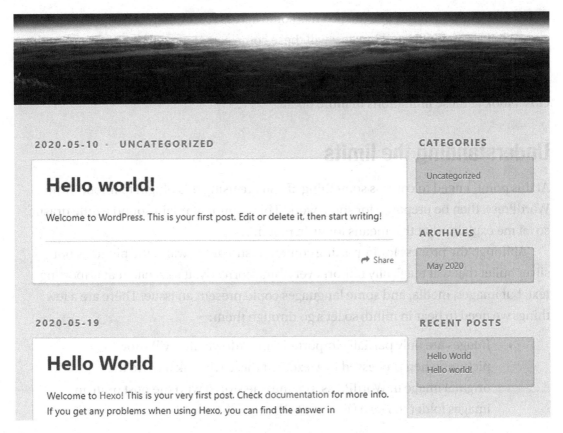

Figure 11-6. *The imported WordPress post, now displayed in our blog*

11. It's worth noting that the post will appear at the bottom – to change it, edit
     the _config.yml file, to remove the minus sign in the order_by: date
     property. It should look like the screenshot shown in Figure 11-7.

```
58    # order_by: Posts order.
59    index_generator:
60      path: ''
61      per_page: 10
62      order_by: date
63
```

Figure 11-7. *The edited order_by property*

At first glance, it looks like the text has come across reasonably well, right? But hold on... What about media and images: will these come across as well? A closer look at the imported content will reveal a few limitations that we must be aware of when using this plugin. It's essential to understand what these are and what this means for us. Let's take a closer look at these limitations in more detail.

Understanding the limits

At this point, I need to confess something: if you are using this plugin to import from WordPress, then be prepared for some work! This comment might sound a little drastic, so let me explain what this means for us in practice.

Although the process for importing content is straightforward, the plugin is not a silver bullet that will magically import everything correctly. It's excellent at importing text, but images, media, and some languages could present an issue. There are a few things we need to bear in mind, so let's go through them:

- Images are only partially imported – markdown files will show pictures when processed by Hexo, but these will link back to the original image in WordPress, not the one stored with the post or in an images folder in Hexo (Figure 11-8).

```
    ::before
▼<p>
  ▼<a href="http://127.0.0.1/wordpress/wp-content/uploads/2020/05/
    cruiseboat.jpg" title class="fancybox" rel="article2">
      <img src="http://127.0.0.1/wordpress/wp-content/uploads/2020/05/
      cruiseboat.jpg" alt> == $0
    </a>
  </p>
```

Figure 11-8. *Console.log shows original links to WP images, not ones in Hexo*

- The plugin won't import any videos embedded in WordPress pages, although you may find that it will show a link to any that were embedded, such as YouTube (primarily because the links would have been in the original page) – as shown in Figure 11-9.

imperdiet dolor. Sed condimentum porta interdum. Morbi euism

https://www.youtube.com/watch?v=aqz-KE-bpKQ&t=5s

A demo video

Figure 11-9. *The results of importing embedded videos into Hexo*

- If you run the process multiple times, then I would recommend clearing out any previously imported files first. The migration process does not allow for individual posts to be selected, so you may find a certain amount of duplication could appear (Figure 11-10).

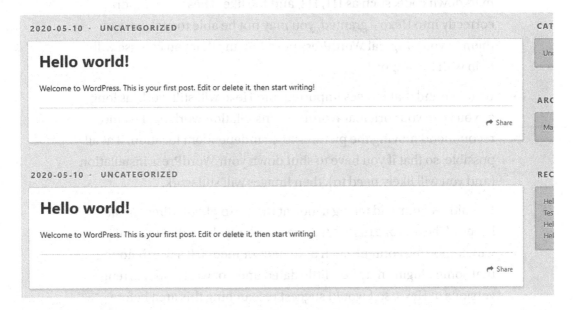

Figure 11-10. *Duplicate posts appearing in Hexo*

- Excerpts are not copied across, at least in their original format – you will likely find that the text will migrate, but that excerpt functionality will need to be re-added.

- The plugin is limited to importing text – my tests show that it will work fine for most languages. However, double-byte languages such as Japanese could be problematic, and you may still have to do some tidying up, depending on how the original text was laid out on-screen.

These limitations may sound like it's creating more work for us, but it's essential to bear in mind that not every export/import process will be perfect. One should always allow for the need to complete a certain amount of tidying up after the initial import process. That said, there are a couple of things that can help ease the burden of importing content into Hexo:

- Where practical, try to keep in mind the types of tags used in markdown code, such as H1, H2, and the like. These will import correctly into Hexo – granted, you may not be able to make use of them in your original WordPress post, but any that you can use will help with the import!

- Bear in mind that images imported into Hexo will still work, as long as you keep your original WordPress installation working. I would recommend moving the pictures to an independent location, if at all possible, so that if you have to shut down your WordPress installation (and you will likely need to), then images will still work.

- I would recommend taking a look at the Hexo plugin directory at `https://hexo.io/plugins/`; there are plenty there that may help you with importing content, such as images or media. It's worth noting that some plugins may be a little dated and not work with current versions of Hexo, so I would suggest researching this area before making any changes.

- Failing this, keep a list of all images used – you can either move them into a central images folder or into asset folders that come with each post or page. You can then do a search and replace on all common link paths, to remove any dependencies on WordPress – you might want to consider putting the images into a central location to start with, to help facilitate the search and replace process!

- Videos (and also audio files) will be problematic – as Hexo won't import any content added through the use of WordPress plugins, you may find you end up with just a series of links. It's worth researching to see if any plugins exist that can detect for the presence of media links and convert them into the appropriate media file. If you have lots of different sources in use, then see if you can rationalize them – this will also help too!

These pointers are just a couple of ways you can help make the transfer process more manageable – it will help to keep the type of tags available in markdown at the back of your mind. It means that any change you make will be more straightforward; ultimately, though, it will require a lot of planning and a degree of effort to complete the migration process.

Okay, let's move on. Time to get a little technical! Although many of you will just want to move content across to Hexo, there will be some of you who will be intrigued as to how the migration process works. Hexo uses the Migrator API, for which the syntax is very similar to helpers or tag plugins that we created earlier in Chapter 5. Let's take a look at this API in more detail, so you can understand something of how it works and use it as a basis for writing your migration plugins for future use.

Using the Migrator API

If we take a peek at the code behind the WordPress migrator plugin from Hexo, it might, at first glance, look a little intimidating! This is particularly so when it features a meaty regular expression string about halfway down – that's enough to scare anyone...

In reality, the code isn't as complicated as it might seem – our plugin is hosted at `https://github.com/hexojs/hexo-migrator-wordpress/`. If we browse to it, it shows a fairly standard file listing for a typical migrator plugin, as indicated in Figure 11-11.

🤖 **dependabot-preview** chore(deps-dev): bump eslint from 6.8.0 to 7.0.0 (#59) ⋯		
📁 test	test: initial commit	
📄 .eslintignore	style: initialize eslint	
📄 .eslintrc	style: initialize eslint	
📄 .gitignore	chore: gitignore package-lock	
📄 .mocharc.yml	chore(deps-dev): bump mocha from 6.2.2 to 7.0.0 (#55)	
📄 .travis.yml	chore: requires at least Node 10.18 (#56)	
📄 LICENSE	Added readme & license	
📄 README.md	docs: update repo name (#50)	
📄 index.js	style: spacing	
📄 package.json	chore(deps-dev): bump eslint from 6.8.0 to 7.0.0 (#59)	

Figure 11-11. *The hexo-migrator-wordpress source at GitHub*

All hexo migrator plugins center around this function, no matter where the plugin is being used:

```
hexo.extend.migrator.register(name, function(args){
  // ...
});
```

This syntax works similarly to other plugins created for use in Hexo – we are effectively extending an instance of the hexo object, which is a direct reference to Hexo. Into it, we register our migrator function; this receives two arguments. The first is the name of the source (in our case, this would be `'wordpress'`) and the second `args,` which represents the user's input from the terminal session (in this case, the location of the XML file).

If we compare this to the source for `index.js`, available at `https://github.com/hexojs/hexo-migrator-wordpress/blob/master/index.js`, we can see how the hexo. extend.migrator function call is used:

```
hexo.extend.migrator.register('wordpress', (args, callback) => {
  const source = args._.shift();
```

This function call starts at line 22, but we begin, though, with several `const` assignments to various helper packages that the plugin uses, before initiating the call to `hexo.extend.migrator`.

It first checks to make sure we have a suitable source for the exported WordPress file; if not, we warn the user. Assuming we do have one, then we begin the real work at 41, where we use the `async.waterfall()` method to work through several functions in turn that first parse the XML content before lifting the text, tags, category labels, and the like and assigning them to the appropriate bucket in our Hexo blog.

Summary

Migrating content from any blog to Hexo reminds me of the phrase that you "can't have pleasure without some pain," at least at some point in a migration process. It has to be said that while Hexo makes exporting content very simple, it is limited in what it can import, so meaning we have some work to do once the migration is complete! We've covered some useful pointers in this chapter around the subject of migrating to Hexo, so let's take a moment to review what we have learned.

We kicked off by exploring the migration process at a very high level; we saw how the technical migration only forms a small part of the overall process. We then took a look at some of the plugins available for performing that technical migration, with a focus on using WordPress as our example blog.

Once we had completed some obligatory housekeeping admin, we then ran through the technical process for exporting and importing content. At the same time, we covered some of the limitations around what we can import and explored some pointers to help make the process easier.

We then rounded out the chapter with a look at how the Hexo migrator plugins work, so for those of us who want to try writing one (or improving an existing one), we can understand the various elements that make up these plugins.

Phew! What a journey! As people often say, all good things must come to an end as we reach the end of this book. I hope this has been an exciting peek into the world that is the Hexo blogging framework and that you've enjoyed getting to know this intriguing tool as much as I have enjoyed writing this book.

Index

A

Application program interface (API)
  blog development, 89
  code generators
    CNAME file, 101
    content, 99
    db.json file, 100
    source code, 101
  configuration options, 103
  core functions, 90, 91
  digging deeper, 102, 103
  extensions, 92–94
  Grunt implementation, 104–106
  helpers
    Google-hosted font, 94
    source code, 94, 95
    style sheets (script files), 93
    use of, 93, 94
  hexo.exit() method, 102
  Node.js, 102
  plugin option, 89, 90
  Sass code
    compilation, 108–111
    package.json file, 111
    renderer command, 108
    working process, 111
  tags snippets
    account plugins, 99
    audiofile.js, 97
    audio tag insertion, 98
    references, 96
    source code, 99
  task runner process, 104–108
  watch() command, 104
Application Programming Interface (API)
  migration process, 249–251
Automation process
  _config.yml file, 149
  confirmation, 151
  content checking, 152–154
  content live, 156
  deployer method, 155
  domain name, 156–160
  GitHub Pages site, 150, 151
  HTTPS encryption, 160
  login screen, 153
  plugin, 149
  review (GitHub), 154, 155
  uploading content, 154
  website online, 149

B

Blogging tools
  creation, 7, 8
  installation, 9
  overview, 1
  WordPress, 2
  workflow (*see* Workflow process)

Printed in the United States
By Bookmasters